The
Heart of the
Cairngorms

For David Craig

- To bend the ear to silence is to discover
how seldom it is there.
Nan Shepherd, *The Living Mountain*

The
Heart of the
Cairngorms

Jim Crumley

Colin Baxter Photography, Grantown-on-Spey, Scotland

First Published in Great Britain in 1997 by
Colin Baxter Photography
Grantown-on-Spey
Moray PH26 3NA
Scotland

ISBN 1-900455-27-7

Printed in Great Britain by The Cromwell Press

Cover Picture © Colin Baxter 1997

The Heart of the Cairngorms

Wildcat

Not as advertised
in spine and claw
and icicle fang

just a pussyfooting
stripey cat exploding
felt-toed the myths

of a bad press.
An easy birchy drift
soft-shoe shuffles

through bracken caress
– ae frond kiss. No hiss
or spit or skirl

nor fur a-bristle
Probably he purrs
himself to sleep

– although admittedly –

he bedfellows at ease
with eagle shadows
and glacial rogues

and when he walks
he swings his tail
like a cosh.

Jim Crumley, Glenmore 1997

Chapter One

A Sure Granitic Space

SPACE. THE VERY WORD sounds like itself. Space in hard white waves, blue at the edges. Space you can walk on, a sure granitic space, consoled and glorified by snow at least four seasons old.

Then, on a July afternoon, the new snow comes, further consoles, further glorifies, enhancing the old midsummer familiarities a thousandfold. The commonplace is rendered sublime. Cloud shadow and sunset fall on these old and new snows and in my head they are the abodes of mountain Gods. The unwary and the unlucky die here...the abodes of jealous Gods.

Somewhere in the last half-hour I must have breasted the 4000-ft contour. I must have head-butted it first, then breasted it, then kicked it apart a few moments later. I see no reason why contours should exist only on land and cheerfully chalk them on to the mountain space as I breathe in its air. What if I inhale at 3999 feet and don't exhale until 4001 feet; is the mountain confused because some of its air is in the wrong place? My little joke to amuse the mountain Gods. Why, then a voice from the cloud shadow in my head points out that the 4000-ft contour as I see it is not the 4000-ft contour as the mountain sees it. It seems I have overlooked the unmeasured vertical miles beneath my feet, those miles down to where the mountain is merely an upstart of the raw stuff of planet Earth. And by the way (the voice grows seen-it-all-before ironic), had I noticed the three different tiers of wind I'd climbed through? And would I like to know how many more there are between here and the nearest cloud? Unless, that is, the mountain Gods stir in a few more before tea, or conjure up their most difficult trick in the high Cairngorms, a flat calm? Oh, and the first of my breathed-out air was below and behind me before the last of it left my lips.

The cloud-voice has made its point. I defer, swear fealty and silence, then burst apart the next contour with particular vehemence.

From where I stand, the shape of the planet makes sense, a so-wide and gently rumpled curve. The summit of Ben Nevis may be higher, but it is not as airy as this. There is no sense there of standing on the summit of the land, and I have never thirled to it. Here is the summit of the land, here the curving edge of the planet, here the substance of space that comes at you in hard white waves, blue at the edges.

Four thousand feet. Among the mountains of Scotland it is a Rubicon of contours, a boundary beyond which lies the most rarefied of all our realms. Up here there is miles of it, miles of hard space, space you can walk on. Four thousand feet is not even a foothill in the Himalaya. But in the Himalaya you have to reach several times 4000 feet before you encounter a world this bare, this hard, this elemental, this basic. And from that single famed Himalayan highspot where there is more space than this, you cannot walk on it.

The 4000 feet of the Cairngorms plateaux are mountain enough for me, summit enough, space enough, rarefied enough. You share your high summer day here with the sun, with its sky, and the wide, crumpled curve of the planet, with cloud shadow and sunset, with new snow and old, and (if you are lucky or your eyes are open enough) with the natives...

...Look at this. There is a shape on the ground, not stone, not tussock, not moss, not lichen. It blinks. So it has an eye, a tiny black jet. That blink tells you which end is which, and once you know that, you can make sense of the shape. Above the eye is a skinny caterpillar of white, an eye-stripe, except that stripes are supposed to be straight. Above the eye-stripe, a black cap, west of the cap, a short stab of black bill, beneath the eye a tufty white cheek, a grey muffler, a white cummerbund, a swathe of peach; east of all that a tumble of all these shades, the haute couture of dotterel, a male, brooding eggs. Now, do this: turn round, close your eyes for ten seconds, open them, turn back, and try and find him again. For perhaps a minute, your eyes flounder among the stones and what passes for grasses at 4000 feet. Damn. He's gone. Then suddenly he leaps into focus. He has been where you left him all the time. It's not easy being a dotterel in the high Cairngorms, living among the waves of space and shrugging off summer snows. So nature compensates with gifts of camouflage and rock-stillness and a lifestyle as exceptional and uncompromising as its surroundings – polyandry. To make the most of the short season of insect plenty on the summits and plateaux and bare shoulders, the female dotterel must maximise her resources – eggs. Conventional nesting practice won't do. Brooding eggs, and loyalty to one mate and one nest are wasteful of dotterel resources, so the tribe goes in for what science calls 'reverse courtship' which is not as painful as it sounds. The female wears the bright clothes, takes several mates, lays in one nest after another, and the male broods the eggs in the muted colours and the rock-stillness. Matriarchy at 4000 feet.

Or...look at this, where the old snow clings to a rim of the plateau, a corrie headwall. The meltwater oozes down into a thousand crannies. A tribe of botanical stoics lives here, hooked up to the drip feed of the snows, plants as specialised and rare as the landscape itself. Brook saxifrages trail across a handful of sodden inches, a life so tentative you wonder why it bothers. But then, for a week or two of this highest of summers, it thinks vertical and thrusts a small white flower an inch towards the sky. The fact that it must thrust up through new snow on a June afternoon will not deter its flimsy mission. Others, like the alpine willow herb, resort to stoloniferous techniques, that is they creep, and to assist the creeping they throw down the gauntlet of a new root every other creeping inch. A feeble stem, skinny rather than slender, wobbles up to a hooded, drooping pink flower. The gesture of defiant life astounds me every time. Alpine flowers stand in the first rank of nature's heroes.

And by what whim of nature's perverse system of logic does thrift of all tide-edge dwellers find a niche right out on the plateau, lustrous pink crowns squatting on the very granite bed of the massif, lifeblood out of a stone? I remember, for example, a vivid cluster of the self-same flowers thickening a lush verge on Gigha's single roadside, a yard above the high tide. Balmy, palmy Gigha and Arctic-alpine Ben MacDhui, and very little in between. I don't pretend to understand, but sometimes it is enough to marvel.

Wherever nature's laws still hold sway, wherever the word 'wild' still fits the landscape's clothes, I have adopted the idea of a single creature to embody the spirit of the place: one presence, one voice, one trait which attunes to the demands of the particular landscape, and endears that tribe to all who walk softly and watch. I think of red-throated divers in Shetland, whooper swans in Iceland, the boisterous St Kilda wren, golden eagles in the Skye Cuillin, alpine lady's mantle (an unlikely emblem I know, but there are no rules) in Glencoe, buzzards in Knapdale, ospreys in a certain wood and watersheet of the Highland Edge, and I know no-one who loves the Cairngorms who does not also love ptarmigan.

In this high summer season, ptarmigan are the shades of the plateau, the broken tones of gravel and screes, the lumpen shape of rocks where they sit and snore, the clarion not of sleep but watchfulness. Sound is as likely to guide your eye to a ptarmigan as anything. Even in movement, running or slow-marching through the boulders, they have something of the naturalness of winds and go undetected. And whereas the dotterel flies in to nest and sits tight and makes do with what clothes it has packed for the journey, the ptarmigan is hefted to the high Cairngorms and dons and doffs the mountains' colours more or less as the mountain does, a rolling programme of moults and mottles culminating in perfect midwinter ermine.

My mind's eye slips back through a clutch of winters to a day in Coire Garbhlach, that twisting, narrowing gouge in the massif's western flank. The snow had made a night of it, binding rocks and smothering slopes. Now, in the morning after, it grew fitful and lethargic, and I walked and scrambled with that rarefied zest with which new snow fuels the journey of the mountain-thirled. I had clambered up on to a rock ledge with a photograph in mind. As I straightened up on a good stance, my eye came level with the cocked heads and blackly penetrating stare of four snorer-birds. The nearest was not six feet away, the furthest no more than eight, and the 400mm lens in my hand was quite useless. So we looked at each other, the two nearer birds crouched into the snow, the two beyond them standing tall to crane over their backs at the sudden appearance of my head from below. The impasse lasted seconds but felt eternal. I knew something like shame because there was nothing I could do – nothing at all – which would not disturb them, whereas anything they did – anything at all – would intrigue and captivate me. My frame of mind skidded awkwardly from hand-in-glove mountain kinship to intruder. They spared my blushes and flew. They climbed and curved round the wider airspaces of the corrie's leaning walls, holding a tight diamond formation. Then, because they were the broken shades and shapes of new snow on old rock, they disappeared as they flew, and I learned for the first time what it means to vanish into thin air.

Only a long spell of winter snowlessness (as rare in the high Cairngorms as a brook saxifrage) betrays the ptarmigan, for then it glows like a midsummer thrift on a gravel bed, and eagle-eyed shadows swoop with gratitude. Ptarmigan trust stillness more than most things. There are those who say you can lift a sitting hen from her eggs. There are those who say that if you do the hand that lifts her should be severed at the wrist. But if you doubt their ability to think for themselves beyond the simplistic principle of stillness, consider this:

October, the heathers and the hill grasses and the heaths wearing smoky shades of fire, not the gaudy shades of lowland autumns but something more muted, embers rather than flames. Seven ptarmigan feed among the berries, leaves and stems of their realm – crowberry, blaeberry, straggles of dwarf willow, the very tips of heather. It has snowed in the night, but in the noon of the morning after, the sun is warm and the wind has blown itself out. Seasons are forever tripping over each other here. The ptarmigan look relaxed, but half a mile away an eagle has just crossed their hill shoulder. The eagle wears the shades of the autumn mountain, the ptarmigan wear their half-and-half plumage, neither summer nor winter. As camouflage goes, it looks impressive enough to me, but I do not see with eagle eyes, and I do not bear the ptarmigan's burden of eagle-wariness. They fly, one hundred yards on a blatantly pre-determined course, then they land on a big scree. At once, it is as if the scree has consumed them. They are rock, and they have its shades and its stillness. The eagle drifts over, looking down, drifts on, working the space, always the space.

The ptarmigan sit among screes. I sit among rocks. I look along the line of their flight. It was fast and direct and flat and it crossed from the slopes above the corrie rim to the screes which burst the corrie rim apart. To follow the corrie rim would be to travel a quarter of a mile from where they took off. By crossing the corrie's highest space, they reduced the distance to a hundred yards.

The nature of space is fourfold on the plateau.

The first is the space which the land itself implies, the wide and undulating miles, higher than anything else other than their own summits which curve up at the edges of the plateau. Not so much summits as the last thrust of the plateau. It is the plateau itself which is the summit, the upper limit of the land, the upper limit of all Scotland bar the distant and isolated slum which is the consummation of Ben Nevis's brute bulk. You see? Ben Nevis is bulk. The

Cairngorms are space. Ben Nevis introverts. The Cairngorms liberate because of the very space the landscape occupies. It is a high place, without imparting the sense of height. To be sure you have to toil to attain the plateau, but it is no Ben Nevis, no Bidean nam Bian, no Sgurr Alasdair which awaits you. It is a high landscape spreadeagled across itself as space, space in hard white waves, blue at the edges, space you can walk on.

The second nature of the space is above you, higher than the extent of your imagination, and curving down in every direction beyond the rim of that first space which is the land itself. So the land is a space within a space, like a rock within a bubble. That second space is the preserve of winds and eagles; I have seen a golden eagle board the high summer thermals here and climb out of sight by going beyond the reach of my eyes, by growing too small to focus on. I wonder how high he can go? I suspect as high as his inclination.

Mostly it is the eagle's airspace, and only the eagle's. But from time to time, at the seasons of migration, there are other travellers following its unmarked trade routes. I have heard for myself the most profound silence I have ever known – heard it here on the plateau – and heard it eventually yield to the high passage of geese. When I found the source eventually, it was a skein heading south at perhaps 7000 feet, and if it thought in its collective wisdom that altitude was a protection against the predation of eagles, it was ignorant of the bird which thermaled beyond the limit of my sight. It is not unknown for a free-falling eagle to strike a flying greylag feet first and follow it down to the plateau. There is a lot of eagle feeding in a goose.

The third nature of space is the one which intervenes, burrowing deep troughs into the cohesion of the massif.

These are places where the roof of the massif – the plateau top itself – has fallen in, borne to oblivion by glaciers. Whenever you stand on a rim of such a trough (the Lairig Ghru is their pre-eminent thoroughfare, Gleann Einich their matchless cul-de-sac), it is not the sudden absence of land which impresses but the swelling presence of space. It rises to meet you in a huge wedge, and it is the most intimidating of all nature's artefacts in the Cairngorms.

My personal anthology of Cairngorms imagery contains nothing more durable than the sight of the Lairig Ghru from the road between Pityoulish and Coylumbridge. The Lairig appears as a perfect V-shaped cross-section from the north, but on that winter afternoon it had been made triangular by a bridge of cloud at 3000 feet. But a fluke of sunlight had holed the cloud and lit the Lairig beneath its cloud canopy, so that its roofed-over wedge glittered yellow. Then as I watched, the cloud began to cave in where it clung to the mountainsides, seethed slowly down the flanks of the Lairig, curved across the floor of the pass and met itself there, so that it left not a wedge-shaped pass but a lit and circular tunnel of gleaming space.

Then the cloud thickened and boiled down, obliterating first the pass then slowly, over an hour, the whole mountain massif. A stranger alighting here after that hour would see the pinewoods of Rothiemurchus tilt gently into a shroud, unsuspecting of all mountains. But even after the grey shutters of cloud were hauled down, I fancied I could still sense the tunnel of space beyond them, still burrowing brilliantly, a slender fluorescence illuminating the hemmed-in thoroughfare of the Lairig.

It was a telling revelation, reinforcing to my utter satisfaction my long-held belief in the idea of the Cairngorms as a single mountain, an entity divided only by fissures in its surface. The Cairngorms do not amount to a range of mountains but a massif wrought from two elements – granite and space. Wherever you wander in the Cairngorms, these are its stupendous constants. The form of the land does not change, nor does the embrace of space. The massif curves and climbs up out of what is left of its forests in shoulders and slabs and corries. However you chance on it, whatever the compass point, there is no mistaking its ambience, its vast extent, its lit and shadowed space. There is only one Cairngorms.

But there is a fourth space.

I had not suspected its presence until I saw the ptarmigan fly fast and flat across the corrie. They neither rose when they took off, nor descended when they landed. They flew across the gulf of the corrie and at my eye level. In their wake they left the sense of their flightpath etched on to a flat disc of space. I had never thought of space as having a surface before, but there it was, stretched across the crown of the corrie from wall to wall, taut as a drum skin, tangible as a mountain loch. If I had gone to the precise rocks whence the birds had flown and squinted down their flightpath to the scree, the surface of their space-disc would have shimmered and bounced back the sunlight.

It is not every landscape which assists such ideas. But the Cairngorms landscape deals only in grand gestures, holds itself in the deportment of cathedrals. In the heights of the great cathedral transepts it is the encapsulated space which impresses too, as much as that which is heaped up stone.

The word 'unique' is as overplayed by conservation as the word 'trust' in a general election campaign. But the Cairngorms merit the word 'unique'. The massif is one of a kind, and we should treat it accordingly. It is granite and space clad in the threads and rags of the ancient filamor that was the Great Wood of Caledon. It is the yardstick by which we should judge all our Highland landscapes, and by the way we treat it and tend to its ailments, the yardstick by which we should judge ourselves in our relationships with wildest nature.

Chapter Two

The Sound of Music

DO YOU HEAR it? If you do, can you believe your ears? Larks don't climb this high, nor wrens, formidable mountaineers that they are (I know wrens which nest higher than golden eagles). This is no place for songbirds. But one just sang.

You look around the bouldery strewment. You have walked for an hour in cloud. You can see 100 yards of cloud in every direction. It is not raining but you are wet. Every rock is darkened by the airy ooze. At times the cloud reels at you like a drunk, coming too close for your comfort. You point the compass at it for reassurance. It tells you what you want to know. A cluster of starry saxifrage (my favourite for no reason that I can put a thought to) stumbles past your right boot. Rocks and lesser stones come at you and veer away. Some rush in under your feet and unbalance you. You step down tentatively for the gravel bed, for the skin of the mountain. You hear your foot crunch into place. In the cloudscape, space is reduced to pockets, bubbles with a 100-yard radius, and the mountain is as hard to the touch as it is unfathomable. You fall back on memory, but you rely on your compass hand. Then a rock sings.

The cloud plays tricks with the sound. You can pin it down to a segment of your space bubble, nothing less than 90 degrees. Somewhere between north and east. You stop to

18

silence your own movements – footfall, jacket-and-trouser rustlings, you try to breathe quietly. The cloud grows loud in your ears. It hisses off rocks. It flops in your face. The sound of the singer eddies like a badly tuned radio. Reception should be better than that up here. Can cloud deflect sound waves? Discuss.

You think perhaps it is your mind which is deflected by the sound. Perhaps there is no songbird. Why on earth would a songbird want to sing up here, up in this coughed-up throwback bit of the Arctic? Arctic. The very word explains all. It is an Arctic songbird. What you are listening to is a cock snow bunting, melisma of wilderness. You hear it, but you can scarcely believe it. Nor can you believe the unseen songster's pull on your emotions.

For a lost hour you have been all the mountain there is. That space you occupy on the plateau has moved according to your demands, placed you perpetually at its centre. There has been no substance other than the stuff beneath your feet, because there has been no distance. The sound of that hour has been the duet of your own noise and the hissing cloud. Even your thoughts were louder than the cloud. Self-containment gets you through such miles. You turn in on yourself. Walking becomes its own existence. Occasionally you play your own mind-games to your own rules, trying to conjure up the image of a better day than this, a different season, a higher sky, so that the mountain where you walk is familiar shapes about the turned-up edges of its space. You work at sustaining your mood, and you relish the challenge the mountain has set you. It is only because you are high on the mountain that the hour has meant anything at all. Lesser mountains don't offer so much high lingering as this. Lesser mountains send you down dipping ridges or up to tiny summits or bowling down blunt shoulders. The plateau holds you high, endlessly, for hours and miles, breadth as well as length, that good and sure granitic space you know is there despite the intruder cloud. And then a rock sings, and your careful mood is scattered ptarmigan feathers in a gale.

You fumble in a rucksack for your binoculars. You had not anticipated needing them. The cloud hisses at them and they are quickly smoared with weet.

You scan the rocks hesitantly. Ten yards or fifty?

You listen harder to the song. It doesn't help. But you find that it grows symphonic in your ears, with the power all the great symphonists share to move you beyond reason. The encircling, canopy-ing cloud creates an astonishing acoustic which corrals your every sense, your very awareness, and gathers it all into an intensity of listening. There is nothing to see, touch, taste or smell. There is only this miracle to listen to. On it goes and on. You root and you transfix. You could die listening to that sound. Then something prods your subconscious, reminds you where you are, and that if you don't do something about it soon, you *will* die listening to it.

But still you have not found the bird. You want to see it – even as you shiver – before you go. The clouds part and admit a low-slung covey of ptarmigan. They land fifty yards away, and in the landing, they dislodge the singer. The song silences, you catch the sense if not the detail of his fluttering shape. His singing rock was hidden from you by another a foot bigger. He reappears on the bigger rock.

He's tiny! His rock is nothing but a pimple on the gnarled and ancient skin of the massif. He is less than the size of a flea on a pimple. He is solid black-and-white, however, in a haze of grey-and-weet. That lets you focus. He stands on his new podium, and he conducts himself. The symphony trembles, then it flows and flows.

The clouds part again. Six people, gatecrashers in uniform Berghaus, stomp loudly through the auditorium, laughter oblivious of the adagio. One notices the audience on his rock.

'Hey. You okay, mate?'

'Fine. Just resting. Admiring the view.'

'Oh. Right. Take it easy.'

The clouds close behind them.

Where did the singer go? The ptarmigan?

Chapter Three

The Stuff of Legend

YOU DO NOT WALK voluntarily into Gleann Einich. You present yourself on the track under Carn a' Phris-ghuibhais and Gleann Einich inhales you.

It had gone gently enough until then; the long walk-in through the pinewoods (the required preliminary to all thoughtful exploration of the massif), the usual pause to readjust the position of the pine which stands alone so that it aligns with Carn Eilrig, then that crucial extra southward mile at the end of which you have begun to sense the change in the nature of the landscape, especially its vertical scale. You have just caught one more first glimpse of one more mountain shape, a huge level slab of mountain thick with spring snow and thrust improbably across the world beyond, the shape of landscape to come, a cornerstone of Braeriach.

It all changes in a dozen strides where the path inclines and rounds one more curve, and the amphitheatrical might of Gleann Einich unwraps. In midwinter when the three mountain walls confronting you are every known shade of snow and ice and a black boil of snow cloud is camped on the Moine Mhor and shot through with eye-wincing slices of heatless sun, it is a sight to freeze your bones. In a midsummer noon it can look as black as night. It could just be my favourite place on earth.

Gleann Einich is a landscape of immense gestures. To the east is Braeriach, which is a bit like saying to the east of the Pacific is America – it's not quite the full story and what you see is rather less than what you get. What you get here is one tumultuous, fractured, gouged and overbearing wall of Braeriach. But there is so much to Braeriach, so many miles of walls and corries, such a sprawl of plateau, so many millions of tons of heaped granite, that it can easily spare a corner of itself to throw a darkly theatrical shadow across the proceedings of adjoining landscapes.

To the south is Coire Odhar, a curving rim of plateau claimed by no famed mountain name, but rather an abyss carved roundly out of the Moine Mhor, the Great Moss, the ultimate Cairngorms space. To the west are Carn Bàn Mór and Sgoran Dubh Mor, swellings in the sweep of the plateau terminated by splendid miles of broken cliffs, and carelessly numbered – rather than named – buttresses.

Loch Einich is the epicentre of all that, and hauls down all their waters. You can leave spring behind you at Coylumbridge and find winter encamped here, cuckoos and icicles, pine-scented breezes and whirlwinds which rock icebergs as they pass. You have crossed a frontier to reach this place, not one which is marked on any map or is even recognisable on the ground, but a frontier of the mind. You have reached deeper into the massif than you thought you were going, reached a point where natural forces hold sway, and a particularly rarefied and elevated tribe of natural forces at that. Their creed is an Arctic one, their instinctive season is winter, their realm is a pared-to-the-bone one, their idea of compromise is a snow-free August, and their patron saint is a giantess, a grotesque totem of granite iconography – A' Chailleach, the Old Woman, and if that loses something of the required sense of demonry in the translation, it is not my translation. She loiters high on the broken edge of Sgor Gaoith, where she breaks the skyline from miles down the glen. She is the possessor of a legend, of course, a clutch of legends, the most persistent of which is that she is locked in eternal combat with a lesser stooge, Am Bodach (the Old Man, inevitably), and that among other uncompanionable traits, they hurl rocks at each other to while away the passage of millennia. Given that the Bodach is a poor specimen compared to her Amazonian physique, her aim is clearly better than his. It is a shame, I think, for I align with Bodach in this conflict: that old hag cost me a pair of crampons. What happened was this:

The writer David Craig and I once spent five days trudging her stormy acres from above and below, trying to pin down the sense of her store of legends, Dave in pursuit of raw material for his subsequent book *Landmarks* (a majestic trawl among the great natural rocks of the world, climber and poet wonderfully wedded to a single purpose), I because his invitation was such a good idea at the time. We ambushed her from above, for she stands beyond the rim of her cliff, at the end of her own scrambly ridge, and our jaws dropped as one. From afar she is merely a pinnacle with a stupid legend. At close quarters she has eyebrow, eye, nose, mouth and a hideously shapeless torso in which the sculptor left everything to the imagination. Queen Ozymandias, and the lone and level plateau stretches far away.

Anyway we marvelled at her, for she was as awesome as she was ugly. If I'd been a Bodach across the loch, I would have thrown rocks at her too, just to knock that supercilious smile-lessness of her shoulders, make scree out of her ribcage, that kind of thing. Then Dave turned to me and asked if I would mind taking her photograph. And I remembered deciding back at base that I wouldn't need the big lens that day, and I remembered putting down the camera to remove the big lens and put on a short zoom, and I didn't remember putting the camera back in the rucksack, and neither I had, and Dave hadn't thought to mention back at base that he'd like me to do her portrait.

The thing rankled. I snatched a couple of winter days a few months later, retraced our steps across the plateau from Glen Feshie, but on that east-facing rim there were treacheries underfoot. The hard snow of the plateau's gentle crest began to insinuate more and more ice into the mix as I walked west. Then, twenty yards from the rim, with the Cailleach still hidden from view, the mix grew lethal. The plateau begins to tilt towards the rim, and the ice was running with water underneath its thick skin. I was immediately certain that I would not be able to get anywhere near the Cailleach, but I unstrapped the crampons from my pack, then made two of the more elementary mistakes of my climbing life. The first one was to put one crampon down on the ice with its rubber spike guard still on. It began to skate downhill at once, heading for the rim twenty yards away. I made one half-hearted lunge for it, and let go of the other crampon, which set off in its wake. To follow them would have been to risk sliding uncontrollably over the edge, bouncing down a couple of hundred feet of rock, then free-falling a thousand feet into the loch. I sat and watched them go. For all I know, the old hag is wearing them, digging them into her long winters.

Dave wrote here so well, he didn't really need the picture.

I first learned of her existence the way I first learned so much of my Cairngorms store before I went rushing off across the massif to see if it could all possibly be true, from the pages of Seton Gordon's *The Cairngorm Hills of Scotland*. It was published in 1925 so it belongs to a kindlier era for the mountain, one unsoiled by the many blights which have afflicted the Cairngorms in the post-war years. It can be naive, and occasionally it can betray its author's Victorian upbringing, but it is among the freshest and least self-conscious things in my bookshelves and it casually unrolls an impressive knowledge of the mountains and an articulate passion for its wildlife. It also dabbles in myth, hence the Cailleach. And after a couple of pages recalling her terrorist activities from here to Mull, Seton Gordon offers this intriguing image:

> But in January and February the storms soon become persistent, and at length both Cailleach and Bodach are encased in a sheet of smooth ice with snow above it, so that they are numbed and helpless, and able no longer to hold converse until the soft winds of spring release them once again from their imprisonment.

So one frozen midwinter day I may tiptoe down her curving ridge, root around her feet for my crampons, scamper back up the ridge and thumb my nose at her while she rages mutely inside her ice prison. But what a hellish vision the day the ice cracks apart and falls from her and she casts her nakedness around her cliff again, looking for an armful of rocks to hurl...

That then, is the nature of the patron saint of the wilderness you have stumbled upon by letting Gleann Einich inhale you, and it is as well to know. As well to know that if you are seduced by the sward beyond the head of the loch on a golden-green June evening when it looks like an illustration for an album cover of something by Greig...that she's up there watching you. And know that if one of her rocks happens to fall short, you are in the firing line.

Her powers seem not to have troubled the shieling folk, however, for their spoor is clear in the grass, the low ruins, the fragments of a long headwall, the usual souvenirs. I have known lingering hours there, so still that the place felt blessed. I have known a north wind flay the loch so that it looked like the Pentland Firth. I have been happier and more miserable in my own company there than anywhere else I can think of, my states of wellbeing or despair manipulated by landscape forces. Never once have I come close to understanding how the shieling folk yoked themselves to such a place for weeks at a time, even summer weeks, for summer at the head of Gleann Einich is no guarantee of any season at all.

When it grows oppressive in my mind, I start to think of where it lies on a spread map of the Cairngorms, the extent and the nature of the land on every side, the rearing Braeriach, the endlessness of the Moine Mhor, the bare, tilting swathes of plateau swaying west from the clifftops to the ramparts of Glen Feshie. In the midst of all that, a great geological thumbprint was pushed down into the raw stuff of the massif, and when the thumb was lifted out again, Loch Einich lay there, pushed down and sunken with a devil woman perched forever on its skyline. When it grows benign, it does so for exactly the same reasons, but I have imported a better frame of mind with me.

It is a truism of the Cairngorms that they appal as many people as they impress. There are many mountaineers who will toil cheerfully on the sodden buttresses of Glencoe and Lochaber or graft themselves like lichen on to the gabbro of the Cuillin but who cannot handle the required psychology of the Cairngorms. I have my good days and my bad days there but my addiction is irrefutable. Every time I pause to realign the solitary pine under Carn Eilrig then move on, something locks into place and I breather easier, move freer, walk closer with nature. It is a confinement rather than a freedom, but it is a limitless confinement. The shieling folk who made their summer encampments with their beasts between the head of the loch and the corrie walls would know that in a way that no-one has known it since. It is no coincidence that the best pasturage for miles around lies in that cut-off fragment of the massif, exempt from every wind other than north, and that north winds are at their most lenient in summer.

There is no other place in the Cairngorms quite like Loch Einich. There are other lochs, but none so incarcerated. There are other troughs but none is so determinedly cul-de-sac-ed. The great passes, the Lairigs, have their introverting days, but they lighten the traveller's burden with the psychology of through routes. Only Coire Garbhlach's astonishing w-shaped incursions east of Feshie are so doggedly one-way, but Garbhlach's scale is one of intimacy, its headwall narrow as a cupboard door, its ambience friendly. There are no demons in the cliffs. Even Glen Geusachan, walled in as it is under Devil's Point (all the demon you could wish for in a mountain shape) relents as it curves north and climbs out of itself to the alone-ness of Loch nan Stuirteag. Loch Etchachan under Ben MacDhui and Derry Cairngorm is a different creature, more moun-taineer by far, and Loch Coire an Lochain high on Braeriach is too rarefied to justify comparison with anything. Loch Einich, though, draws mysteries into itself in a way that no other fragment of the Cairngorms does, and now that the shieling folk are history pages and the Cailleach is uncommunicative (other than the vitriol she hurls at the Bodach with the rocks), the loch keeps its ancient knowledge to itself.

Seton Gordon bemoaned the all-but-extinction of the legend-bearers of the Cairngorms. Seventy-five years later, their extinction is complete, for they began to fade when Gaelic began to fade as the first language of the landscape, and they died when the language died. The fact that – to a degree at least – the language has begun to resurrect has not been enough to save the legends. You can read them, of course, in the old books, or new books born out of someone's academic obsession. But legends ceased to be legends when the crucial word-of-mouth continuity of the legend-bearers died out, that continuity which kept the stories so alive that every new generation of ears never knew whether or not to believe or scoff, and it didn't matter. What mattered was that the new ears swallowed them whole as legends, learned them well, made them their own with their own variations and embellishments and re-presented them in time for one more generation's new ears.

It is not that the source material, the eager clay from which legend is fashioned, is not still everywhere in the Cairngorms. It is not that you cannot sit gasping and sweating on a misted flank of Gleann Einich, suddenly unsure of your bearings as the wind tugs the sky down and smothers every reliable landmark. And before you reach for the compass and plot your way back into the glen, you might pour a coffee or swig a dram while you breathe in the scents of autumn and look idly back at the trail your boots have just brushed in the sodden tawny understorey of the hillside. If the coffee or the whisky is particularly good, and the coming and going of mountains through the opening and closing shutters of the falling sky is intriguing enough, and if your mind begins toying with the legend-bearers who dwelt on the fringes of Seton Gordon's memory, which made them old in the last quarter of the nineteenth century, and perhaps it was their grandparents they learned them from, so maybe the same legends were clattering around the glen's bothies when Culloden was still future rather than desperate history...

There was, for example, the story of the stalker who was so lost and storm-bound for days in Gleann Einich that he pronounced he had wandered to the sea and back, when what he had seen was Loch Einich in a rage, a rage doubtless fermented by the sorcery of the Old Hag on the cliffs, and doubtless too, she had inveigled her sorceries into the poor benighted oaf's mind.

Half-truths are irresistible seductions. When storm unprecedented in living memory confronts unparalleled landscape like the high Cairngorms, almost anything can be proclaimed as if it really happened, and slip effortlessly into the usage of legend. But what really happened? He didn't really see the sea, did he? No stalker could travel seventy or eighty miles beyond the mountains and not know he had left the mountains, even seventy or eighty miles in a sightless storm, a fog, a whiteout...but some scrap of reality, tortured by extremes of circumstance, was the foundation of what it was he said he saw.

I am unlikely ever to tire of recreating in my mind a trick of light I encountered near the Pools of Dee in the Lairig

Ghru, travelling through fitful March snow showers and just as fitful sunlight. The wind was at my back so that the snow seemed to rush past me, sometimes grey and unlit, sometimes dazzling fragments of yellow-gold when the sun was on them. But up at the watershed, they seemed to hit a contrary wind, and there they swithered and crowded and thickened. Then, as if a switch had been thrown, the whole width and height of the pass was full of rainbow colours, a shallow arc first doubled then trebled, but inside the mountain walls, not against the sky, a three-tiered snow-bow. Now if I had come on that illumination after two or three stormbound nights out on the mountain, lost and terrified and havering, I might well have suspected that I had died somewhere back down the Lairig and I was about to see the Pearly Gates.

What was the stalker's revelation on Loch Einich? Some fluke of sightlines – a tiny gap in the cloud with the moon in it? – which he translated as a lighthouse and stitched on to the very real surf-like crash of Loch Einich's waves, allied to the trickery of storms severe enough to confound all sense of time and distance? Doubtless when he was home and dry and fed and watered he would make the most of it, and be convincing enough because of what he believed he saw. And because storying was once a crucial component of Highland nights, the story would repeat and repeat and it would travel, with or without its author. Before the winter was out it was halfway to legend. Over a couple of centuries it would be embedded deep in legend's mainstream, and barely recognisable from the stalker's ordeal.

So I was sitting and gasping and sweating on a misted flank of Gleann Einich, unsure of my bearings, and the wind tugged at the sky and I swallowed first coffee, then whisky, and every reliable landmark was lost. I listened to the hill sounds while I played mind-games with half truths. I heard the wind in the rocks high above the watershed where I sat. I heard tumbled water. And from fluctuating distances and directions I heard the hoarse operatics of the red deer rut. It was a small pass where I sat, of no consequence in the mountain roll-call of passes, but known to the deer as a route between grazings or a deflector of storms. The sky edged closer and lower.

A kestrel cruised into my airy nook. He wheeled twice, planed along a small crag, stood off my own rock at my eye level for perhaps ten seconds, then fell. He checked, fell again, checked again, then thumped softly into the grasses where he so closely matched the autumn colours that it looked as if the hill had reclaimed its own temporarily dislodged fragment, like a golfer replacing a divot. He rose vole-taloned and burrowed into the clouds.

Rain fell, and with it fell a kind of imposed lethargy. I should at least be back down on the glen track before dark, but I felt less and less like moving. I sat, and my thoughts grew ragged and confused. Then an eagle replaced the kestrel. He was flying along the mountainside, rather than across the watershed, so slow and so low to the ground that he appeared more a thing of the mountainside than the air, walking on his wingtips. He rose a few feet when he reached the watershed, then not twenty yards away, and again at my eye level, he reached up to a second rock and perched. So we sat on our rocks, either side of the watershed, like finials on gateposts, and an old stag walked between us and below us.

The sounds of the rut had grown faint over the last half-hour. Its nearest skirmishes had moved down on to the lower ground as the weather worsened. Here was a stag which had been ousted from the rut. The fall of an old master stag is one of the most pathetic of nature's spectacles. He stumbled through the curtains of cloud and he was bloodied by the rut. He was going east when the rut was west, a dethroned monarch, too heavy, too slow, too old. A great roar rose from unseen slopes below. He stopped on the watershed, turned his head to the sound but he could not muster the guts to roar back. That would have provoked confrontation. I wished him a placid and brief exile.

He turned again and crossed the watershed, began the descent into the eastern corrie. At that moment, the eagle slipped off his rock and resumed his slow flight, but now he too crossed the watershed, following the stag a little to his left, like an outrider on escort duty. For a dozen yards before I lost sight of them, they kept pace with each other, then as they disappeared, I suddenly remembered my friend Mike Tomkies's description of the golden eagle as 'nature's dark angel of death', and although this wasn't quite what he had in mind when he wrote that, the form of words was chillingly apt...the angel of death escorting the stag on his last journey...

On an impulse, I took a scrambling detour down the crag to close on the stag and watch his descent to the east. I came into the lee of another rock and found him twenty yards away. The eagle was not in sight. The stag stepped beyond a slight rise in the ground and I followed. His tracks gleamed wetly on a yard of deer path, but when I inched round one more rock with the wind in my favour, there was nothing. The path led down into a wide bowl of heath and rock and rough grass. He was not there. He was not in the bowl. In the last hour of daylight, the sun suddenly began to spear into the corrie, the clouds began to shred and peel back, the rain ceased, the mountain glittered. I saw the eagle again, quartering the lower slopes of the corrie, then perch on a pointed rock. The sun lit him where he sat, no longer a dark angel of death but a bronzed gargoyle bird. I have come on that rock often since that day. It always looks from a distance as if there is an eagle perched on it, but there never is.

The pinewoods reel you in again, then, but you walk more thoughtfully now, more appropriately. You watch the trees slide past as individuals. You listen harder, unravelling the bird voices. You are reading nature better. You grow eager for the next mountain glimpse. You step from the track more often to watch a tree creeper, a red squirrel, an anthill. You scrutinise flocks of capering tits for another crestie, and you carry his voice in your head. And now you don't just sense the mountains, you sense them growing near. Then the world changes with a singular spectacular jolt.

The trackside pines stop abruptly.

Space and light lather the land under sun and sky.

Winds breathe easier, bearing new scents.

Pass the last pine and the mountains rush forward. Having rushed they lounge across all the skyline there is. The northern gape of the Lairig Ghru is massively defined, an upturned mountain shape itself, and you see it again as you saw it the last time you stood here, not as a gulf which divides the Cairngorms but as a space which binds them. Read nature. Learn.

You have the lie of the land from here. The track has climbed and borne you to the top of a wide clearing which tilts its skin of heather and juniper away from you towards a dark green sea, a sea where mountains wade on the far shore. A sea full of treetops. Its name is Rothiemurchus, the Broad Plain of the Firs, and it is a glimpse of history, a living souvenir of the Great Wood of Caledon. But you can see its edges, a thing the Great Wood only permitted near its sea coasts. Still, that glimpse reinforces the relationship between pine and granite, tree and mountain, and locks it into your mind as something indivisible. Now, when you have tramped another mile or two of increasingly random trees, and you come on that tree that stands alone, you work your eyes instinctively until you align it under the summit of the first shape to throw a mountain shadow on your footfall – Carn Eilrig.

Carn Eilrig's aloof stance creates illusions of grandeur. If the clouds are down on the comatose massif, its elegant cone seems pitched a further thousand feet up the sky than you remembered it, and if it happens to be wearing a skull-cap of snow, it can rear like Fujiyama. Yet on the clear-skied days when the massif is an endless bulk, Carn Eilrig shrinks, eases back down into the raw stuff of the total mountain, as camouflaged as woodcocks.

It is a curious name for an out-on-a-limb mountain. An eilrig is a narrowing defile, often artificial, for trapping (and usually shooting) deer. A modern one, made of wood, has been used to great effect to reduce deer numbers on Creag Meagaidh on Loch Lagganside. It is difficult to detect such a feature in the landscape of Carn Eilrig. There are, to be sure, two conspicuous 'defiles' in sight, the Lairig Ghru itself, and the passage of the Beanaigh Bheag burn down the monstrous flanks of Braeriach. But they are hardly deer traps. Perhaps in the days of Gleann Einich's long lost population, the natives contrived a deer trap under the mountain. Perhaps not. It is, whatever the source of its christening, the best place I know to step up on to and reacquaint myself with the high Cairngorms, eyeball to eyeball, a place to repossess sensations and read the nature of that unique land.

Chapter Four

To Possess Sensations

THE TREE STANDS alone. The tree stands for its own race. It is its own metaphor and its own monument. Scots pines are down to the last one per cent of themselves, all that remains of the forest that was. The tree which stands alone is the several-millionth part of the one per cent. It makes you think. How many trees were there in the Great Wood of Caledon?

The answer is 'enough'. Enough to render the Highland heart impassable, enough to succour wolves, enough to clothe the massif of the Cairngorms on all its flanks to perhaps 2500 feet. Imagine what that looked like. I try often. Round in the corrie called Creag Fhiaclach you can still get the feel of it. There the forest clings all the way up the head-wall to 2000 feet, then it puts its head over the parapet and meets the wind hurtling down from the plateau. At once the trees thin and flatten. Whether you are pine tree or ptarmigan, snow bunting or mere mortal, the wind is the Cairngorms' great leveller.

Sometimes a single tree is as potent as a corrie-full of trees. Here is a case in point.

The tree is lopsided. It is an aesthetic assessment of course. The tree is perfectly balanced for its own requirements and there is no such thing as symmetry in pine trees, but its south burgeons better than its north. The lowest branches begin one third of the way up the trunk, and they lean south. The north-facing branches begin halfway up the tree and reach out half as far as the lowest south-facing ones. The trunk is straight, but in its very last gesture, its bottle-green crown, it lifts a finger to the north, a slender counterweight to the southward bias of its foliage, north to the Arctic, a pointed fingerpost indicating the direction of the landscape's roots.

The tree seems to commend itself to me as I pass. Alone-ness is part of the appeal, for my own alone-ness is my preferred way through the landscapes of the Cairngorms. Such a tree also signposts my years through the glen, talis-man and undemanding companion for as long as I care to pause. I am apt to converse with her. (She is female in my mind which is probably wishful thinking, or perhaps it is her capacity to endure.) She told me once when we were comparing pedigrees that she could trace her ancestry back to the Ice Age in thirty generations. I was impressed by that.

She has not always stood alone, of course. The corpses of comrades – or at least their bleached and still-rooted head-stones – commemorate the conviviality of the lost forest. They stand all around, or they lie where they fell. But her own survival is intact. She stands on a low ridge, which con-fers status on her beyond her dimensions, as if the landscape had made a plinth of itself for her and set her on it. So you see her from below as you pass on the path into the glen, but you do not see her set against the sky. Instead, the landscape has also given her a mountain-shaped canvas to paint herself on, and it is that which is her ultimate dis-tinction, that which singles her out from her forest bedfellows.

The mountain shape is the profile of Carn Eilrig which is

as solitary in the Cairngorms' scheme of things as the tree. Carn Eilrig stands uniquely apart from the massif, severed by a moat of space as deep as the mountain. It is a lowly shape by the standards of Cairn Gorm and Braeriach which it contemplates, but like the tree which keeps it company, it summarises its own landscape, the Cairngorms in microcosm. It climbs from a thin frieze of Rothiemurchus trees through first heathery then bouldery phases to its own bare and gravelly plateau top. And – as with the great massif itself – the flanks of Carn Eilrig have only space for company. It is as if nature has made a tiny scale model of what it had in mind, left it lying around for reference while it built the real thing, then forgot to tidy up after itself, and left its prototype to its own devices.

One tree, one mountain, pine needles and granite. Be fruitful and multiply. For long enough, they did just that, until first the ice and then the unconcern of people began to unpick it all at the seams.

I like to walk until I set the tree against the mountain, the dark green against the dark grey (or the white if it is winter), and by virtue of the changing sightline from the path below, move the tree until it aligns perfectly beneath the summit of the mountain, and make of that painterly composition a symbolic harmony of pine and granite and (unseen because of my foreshortening viewpoint) the space between them which binds. I like what I have done with mountain and tree over the years, the way I have made them dance to a tune in my head. There is that point in the evening after a long day up among the plateau spaces, or ferreting about the corries of Braeriach, when the tree comes into view, but while I have been supping with the mountain Gods, it has wandered off on assignments of its own. See how far it has gone

astray from the centre of the mountain! So I have to come on
it from a certain direction, like a good collie penning a trou-
blesome ewe, and fix it with my collie's stare until it gives
in and goes and stands where I want it to.

I stand and admire my two symbols of the Cairngorms,
their profound simplicity of form, and looking at them is
suddenly not enough. I want to have a Cézanne's control of
their pointed imagery, to extend a Cézanne's arm towards
the tree and measure it with a Cézanne's thumb. I want to
turn on Carn Eilrig the eyes with which Cézanne beheld his
Mont St Victoire. Sometimes I don't think my own eyes see
enough in that monumental simplicity. I have looked at it. I
have photographed it. I have written it down into a hundred
corruptions of its simplicity.

Cézanne said:

'Be a painter, not a writer or a philosopher!'

Easy for you, Paul, with your eyes, your thumb. I have to
read nature then rearrange the words.

To read nature is to see it, as if through a veil, in
terms of an interpretation in patches of colour
following one another according to a law of
harmony...It is all summed up in this: to possess
sensations and to read nature.

To possess sensations and to read nature! I'll settle for that
as a basis for writing my mountain and my tree, even if I
can't paint. I'll settle for it as a way of life for that matter.

Tree and mountain are indivisible in my mind. Pine trees
are as fundamental to the Cairngorms as granite and fat

wedges of four-seasons-old snow in August. You cannot possess all the sensations at your disposal and read all the nature implied in that mighty coupling of words, 'The Cairngorms', unless you insinuate your presence on the mountain by way of the tree. The pinewoods are a filter capable of purging away all manner of impurities so that the would-be climber is befitted to climb, a necessary overture to the alpine symphony of the mountain so that you hear the purity of its themes and the subtle shifts of its movements, possess its sensations, read its nature free from the encumbering baggage of lesser lands beyond. If you drive to a car park halfway up the mountain and ascend the rest by ski-lift (and it seems as I write that the purgatory of a funicular railway has achieved an unstoppable momentum), you have by-passed the required rites of acclimatisation. In a land which is compressed and clamped down between the sea and a little over 4000 feet, no-one has the right to tread the rarefied spaces of the summit without strenuous endeavour. In the particular circumstances of the high Cairngorms, you must not only climb, you must also walk in, tramp the good green miles of the pine woods, possess sensations and read nature there first.

It matters. If we learn to take the roof of the land for granted, we have kicked away its foundations and the crucial buttressing of corrie walls. The mountain is no longer itself, but a throwaway thing made casual as a coach trip to Santa Claus Land. We have the knowledge to put a railway up the mountain. We have the knowledge, too, to remove every trace of our own blemishing from the face of the mountain, to tend its wounds and let it heal. It's still a choice.

Each time I go back to the Cairngorms, I head first for Carn Eilrig. The route is designed to acclimatise, not by me, but by nature. Nature's first response to my footfall on the pinewood floor is to slow it down. Read nature. It is saying 'Too fast!'

So you walk more slowly, and because you walk more slowly you walk more softly. You are at once less of the outside world, more of the pinewood. Nature gathers trees round you, thickens the density of the wood so that sight-lines shorten and (once you are slow and soft enough on the pinewood floor) you begin to possess sensations. If it is a sunlit wood, you see how the sun makes shades out of the pervasive bottle green from black to blue to yellow, and none of them is not green. The shadows are hard, not like the dappling of oakwoods, and they lie like dark lace on the wood, each tree shadowing several of its kin. There are no pale shades. Juniper rounds out the spaces between trees, in shrubby clumps wading through rich thick understoreys of heaths and mosses. A tiny black-and-white face draws a bead on you from a low branch, monochrome made gaudy by the upstart of a chequered crest. A thin four-syllable piping, pitched in that register of music more suited to the ears of dogs, confirms the encounter. The bird is a crested tit, a pinewood specialist, and its presence lets you know where you are. You have stopped to admire, to possess one more sensation. You are learning what you must re-learn each time you go back.

Pinewoods – good ones like this – have many densities from something like a chaotic plantation to something like parkland to the last high and sparse scattering. Nature slows you again with the first bit of something-like-park-land, a new kind of space to contemplate, space punctuated by rounded giants of pines, stands of waving birch – a pale shade at last – and dragging your eye past them all, the first glimpse of mountain, folds of hugely blunt and dark-red shapes. The forest closes in again, but from that moment on, you walk with the possession of the greatest of all sensations, the knowledge of the mountains, the shape and shade of them unseen but sensed beyond the serried shapes and shades of the pines.

Pinewood Interrogation

If you had stood here
while the Ice whittled
mouthfuls out of mountains tossing
and catching hundred-ton rocks
the way you catch peanuts
in *your* mouth would you
have predicted pine trees
or waist-high mountains

made by ants?

Or...envisaged
capercaillies?
Capering cresties?
Or...trout
dying high and dry, slung
under an osprey's ponderous arc?

Yet it all came to pass
and my last question
is this:

How come?

Chapter Five

The View from the Carn

THERE ARE DAYS when I want to hold the mountains at a distance, not rush to the eager embrace of Lairig or corrie or plateau skies, but go quietly through the pines, and turn aside, and sit and watch, admire and marvel. I was taught by a friend who knows about such things to be selective in an art gallery, just look at one or two pictures and give them time, and go back and look at them again, and again. In that way, he was able to demonstrate to me, he had finally unravelled the compositional structure of a Titian in the National Gallery of Scotland. He sent me a triumphant postcard of it with a sheet of tracing paper attached, explaining his discovery in a few bold diagonals. On the back of the card, the explanation: 'It's triangles!' He was no meagre artist himself, in stained glass and mosaic, and he was not above punctuating the swirls of his mosaic murals with fossils. Two of his small slate mosaics hang above my writing desk, robust and rough-hewn things at first glance, but because my eyes linger over them during pauses between phrases, sentences, paragraphs, chapters, every working day, I have unearthed their intricacies and their compositional strengths. Here and there, for example, stacked slivers of thinly cut slate betray his Orcadian lineage, and the horizontal banding of both pieces acknowledges the artist's debt to Mark Rothko.

I mention it all because the comtemplative nature which I occasionally bring to bear on such a sculpture as the Cairngorms has been hugely informed over the years by countless conversations with George Garson, and whether they are in Gleann Einich or Orkney, his beloved Pentlands or an elite selection of Edinburgh howffs, they invariably home in on the common ground between art and nature. And if that sounds too po-faced and erudite for a book about mountains, you have never eavesdropped on one of our whisky-garnished pie-and-mushy-peas assessments of the correlation between mountains and cathedrals, the grand gestures of nature and man, in Bert's Bar. It is not possible to be pompous with a mouthful of mushy peas.

It is no coincidence that George Garson has been one of my life's few companions among my mountain travels, nor that we have butted in on October winds in Gleann Einich together.

So when I choose a day to hold the mountains at a distance, and clamber alone up to an airy perch for the purpose, it's unlikely that I will sit for long without raising the hipflask to the man who taught me a lot about the art of contemplation.

On such a day, I want to weigh up the place of the Cairngorms in my affection. I want to sit for a long time and smile at the massif, compose odes to its praises and recite them aloud (then eat them in case anyone else should find them – they are not odes for other eyes!). I want to recompose the shape of the massif in my mind, re-examine the mountain shapes within the shape. Robert Louis Stevenson was inclined to do much the same thing (which is excuse enough for me!) with his Edinburgh skyline, that half-built, half-wilderness confrontation between the Castle and

Arthur's Seat. He too would go looking for a place to sit and weigh up their place in his affections, compose odes, etc...

> Of all places for a view, Calton Hill is perhaps the best; since you can see the Castle, which you lose from the Castle, and Arthur's Seat, which you cannot see from Arthur's Seat.

Exactly! The one place in the Cairngorms which precludes a good view of the sense and shape of Braeriach or Ben MacDui, or the way they sometimes lean over at each other, and sometimes recline away from each other, is on the summit of one or other. So I found myself a Calton Hill – Carn Eilrig.

Carn Eilrig transforms itself as you climb. Its compact cone, which is the face it presents to the pinewoods, elongates into a good ridge, stretching south. I like to board it from its southmost dip, hauling myself up from the river with handfuls of funicular heather. And oh the rarity of that particular species of joy which stems from climbing a hill with no beaten path to its summit. The trampling feet in the Cairngorms are elsewhere.

This wholly unnecessary habit of grabbing handfuls of heather to ease the passage over steep ground (and long heather) produced one bizarre consequence on Carn Eilrig. I was climbing rhythmically and well and the May sun was on my back and my mind was God-knows-where, when I reached for a handful of heather which I noticed from a yard away was dull and yellowish. It was the curious notion that I thought the heather might be dead, and therefore not trustworthy to haul on, which stopped me from picking up an adder. It was a lightly coiled female – at roughly two feet, about six inches longer than the male – and as she raised her head lazily into the strong sun I saw the black slit of her pupils close so that it looked as if she was quite blind. She was probably pregnant and unwilling to move if she did not have to. I took a careful step backwards, gave her a wide and quiet berth, then when I was above her and my shadow wouldn't trouble her I sat and watched her for a few minutes. It is not an opportunity which arises every day. She was the third adder I had ever seen in the Cairngorms, all of them in and around Gleann Einich, if you don't count the one I watched lying on a rock for ten minutes before I realised there was no snake inside and that I was looking at a shed skin. She was a rich matt yellow, but the black zigzags down her back were glorious. The more I looked at her, the more I thought she was not yellow at all but gold. It was the first time I considered a snake beautiful. No sooner had the thought crossed my mind than her head went up as though she had read my mind and decided a 'who me?' pose would advance her cause. It did precisely that.

Heather moors are in retreat all across the country. There are countless arguments to resist that tide and I have advanced many of them over the years. With the adder I almost hauled from its beauty sleep, I found another. It is, I think, one of the most persuasive.

There was an old spring, the glen's new growth stymied under two feet of snow, and a curious narrow trail among the usual signatures of fox and hare. I puzzled over it, wondering what kind of creature was so delicate of stature that its feet left no footprints, yet its tail was so lush that it swept away all lingering traces. Then I saw where the trail ended. It ended on a sun-smitten rock, where a small silver-and-black coiled something-or-other glittered on the snow, and that too was an adder. It was the first one which turned my head and made me look at them without the unthinking loathing and fear which my own species tends to heap on the adder tribe. Yes, its bite is poisonous. Yes, it has been known to kill a very few unlucky people but only because it has been disturbed and won't take the wrong kind of disturbance lying down. If it can't escape (its first instinct) then it will defend. But the venom is designed for killing things it eats – voles, mice, lizards, that kind of thing. It does not eat people, even bits of people. And contrary to the cannibalistic myth which human superstition has conferred on adders, neither do they eat their own young. Mostly they go quietly about their own business, and like all the wildest tribes of our native wildlife, they act out of character only when people threaten to trample their wellbeing underfoot.

Carn Eilrig grows bare as its ridge climbs, and the mountain massif is suddenly just that – massive. The summit is broader and rockier than you expect, and as bare as the high plateau. And you have added two crucial dimensions which assist your contemplation of the massif. One is height. The summit is rather more than half as high as the Cairngorms giants, and that altitude puts the big summits and the roots of the massif in their place, and lets you peer deep into the mountain innards of corrie and pass. The second dimension is the intervening space which isolates Carn Eilrig from scoops and slabs and the great mass of the high plateau, its rims and its walls.

And because that space stretches not only from Carn Eilrig to the mountain walls but also *into* the mountain by way of the Lairig Ghru which leans up towards Carn Eilrig's eastern slopes, your rock seat has accomplished something very rare: it has opened up the *depth* of the mountain. Carn

Eilrig's sightline into the Lairig is angled in such a way that you see only the western wall of the pass, corrugated with rock and old snow, something sturdy in monochrome, all sinews and ribs. Or it reveals the fossilised imprint of an adder the length of the Lairig Ghru which slithered south some Ice Age or other, bellying flat out for the sea. It is dangerous to let poetic instincts loose in landscape like this.

I love this summit in the endless sequence of snow conditions which forever beset the Cairngorms, when the big snows have begun to melt, perhaps the highest snowcaps are intact, but elsewhere the mountain is bursting apart the snow chrysalis, something monstrously emergent. The hard edges of rock show through first, the gully beds last. But for a moment, the massif is held in a kind of tense equipoise, a gargantuan pause, while nature scratches its head and wonders what to do next. For that moment, the massif is not itself, neither snow nor rock shaded, but two glimpses at once – of what it was a few days ago and what it might be a few days from now. You sense great forces gathering. You scan the sky: sluicing rains or one more flourish of the Cairngorms' old favourite, winter?

It is good to be on Carn Eilrig, too, when the cloud is down on the massif, down to say, 3000 feet. In that circumstance, Carn Eilrig magnifies to a great isolationist mountain – a Schiehallion! – and suitably elevated beyond its station it feels a more confident wedge of its own landscape. I look over at the Lairig – nothing but a hint of its dropped jaw survives. Behind the drawn curtain of the skies, you have to rely on memory and the sense of the mountain mass, a collage of the biggest shapes in the land – and the most durable – and obliterated as if they had never been by something as ephemeral as a cloud.

Patience, a good deal of luck, a bit of shivering, occasional recourse to the flask, and a quite unwarranted faith in the weather forecast, occasionally conspire memorably. I have seen – from the same Carn Eilrig – the Cairngorms unwrapped. It began with a hole in the cloud through which I could see a scrap of dark angles – Lurcher's Crag, unmistakable even in isolation. Then, the way a snagged jumper can unravel in rather more time than it took to put together, the thing began to fray, and as it frayed it began to lighten. I felt the wind stir from the west, then felt it quicken, and guessed that if it was stirring and quickening here, at 4000feet it was barging bits of cloud apart, and what it couldn't barge it would prise and punch, fistfuls of wind the size of empty corries.

Sun poured. But it poured as if it was being decanted from a watering can, in thin beams which splashed on to the rock and the shards of old, clinging snow. Now the wind was under the skirts of the cloud and causing mayhem. That limp, unyielding hemline, that hodden, homespun grey was suddenly as frisky as a dancer's kilt. Shoulders bared, corries reshaped themselves and stepped forward into their accustomed positions. One by one, the view from the Carn unclothed all the old mountain familiars, until within an hour the mountain was as naked as the day the Ice moved out. Carn Eilrig grew warm and still.

But the thing was not done yet. In the south where Carn Bàn Mór gathers a few folds of the Moine Mhor into an easy summit above the headwall of Coire Odhar, a vast black hood of cloud was massing. I did not much care for the cut of its jib, but confident that I could run before it if the need arose, I sat on to watch its advance. The rocks around the Cailleach's abode were brewing their own clouds, slender white streamers which drifted across the high black stuff with the sun still on them, so that they glowed as bright as the old snow. These searing white Cailleach-clouds drifted a bridge across Loch Einich (I imagined the Cailleach and the Bodach strutting out from their clifftops to meet in the middle for one more bout of hostilities and mutual abuse, each one followed by a retinue of acolytes and trainers with towels round their necks and mysterious buckets to spit into). A tendril of that white cloud crept into a corner of Coire an Lochain on Braeriach, a tentative explorer. But, like an adder on a lizard, the corrie clamped jaws on it and swallowed it whole. Then that three-ringed circus of corries (Coire an Lochain, Coire Ruadh, Corrie Beanaidh – Carn Eilrig is their exclusive box seat) began to juggle with scraps of shining cloud, tapping them from foot to foot, nudging them off knees, shoulders, heading them from headwall to headwall. They passed thickening streamers to each other with the same mesmerising dexterity, but as the streamers thickened and lengthened they began to grow dull and run into each other. At last, a curtain the colour of white fog was drawn across all three corries and the show was done.

I turned back to watch Loch Einich, but it was gone. The black hood had slipped down over its crags and smothered its silver surface. The storm was blundering up the glen and creeping up Coire Dhondail on to the Braeriach plateau. I felt something like a wall of cold air hit Carn Eilrig, and seconds later the first snow flakes. I snatched the mountain jacket from my pack, stowed the flask, shouldered the pack and took Carn Eilrig's steep north slope at a heady run, slithering among rocks, then heather then juniper and pine runts, but I was still well above the river when the serious snows caught up with me. I plunged on, just one more moving fragment of the storm. I glanced up to where the Lairig Ghru should have been, but the black hood was there too, and that crucial space which I had celebrated from the summit of Carn Eilrig was thick and fibrous with falling snow.

I crossed the river by a fallen tree, scrambled up the far bank to the Lairig track, paused for breath, looked back to where the mountains had been, turned again and walked thoughtfully down into the good green benison of the pines.

Chapter Six

The Roe and the Red

IT WAS A SMALL and sunlit clearing where the roe deer met the red squirrel. The clearing owes its sunnyness to the fact that one end of it opens on to the river. It is so deep into the pinewoods that you begin to get an idea of what a true pine forest might feel like. Apart from the dark Glenlivet-brown of the river (a good 12-year-old Glenlivet, aged in oak casks of course) and the glimpses of sky, this is a green place. Pine green, birch green, juniper green, and underfoot moss green and heath green. The further back into the clearing you let your eyes drift, the more yellow the green becomes, but even the yellowest green is irredeemably green. The roe was already there when I arrived, an old doe still in her winter coat although it was early April. So she was dark brown and wore a grey collar on her pale throat. She browsed with her back to me, and sun and shadow fell across her back, and she enjoyed a tranquil respite from that long, long Cairngorms winter. It had been brutal as well as long, and today was the first in the pinewoods to imply that perhaps winter would not last forever, that there would be another spring. Robins dared snatches of flutey song. Tree pipits fizzed up and down their fixed ropes of air, abseiling fast and singing. But these were all that broke the woodland quiet.

I found a comfortable niche across the river from the

clearing, so that the sun was on my back and the roe was beautifully lit. I unpacked camera and telephoto lens and waited.

Over half an hour the roe inched nearer the water. Once or twice I tried speculative compositions as she moved, but I liked none of them. I have all the roe deer pictures I am ever likely to need, but if she would care to step a little closer and into that patch of rich shadow with the yellow light behind her, I would have one more which would be worth the wait. I waited. She stepped closer and browsed on.

The river was in full voice and running high, well fuelled by endless rains and snows, and hurtling by close to the top of its natural banks. The red squirrel came to drink. He was on the roe's side of the river. He paused halfway down, feet splayed, tail flattened above him and pointing straight up the tree. He looked round, then scrambled down, bounced over a yard or two of open ground to the edge of the river then stopped. The water thundered past, inches from his nose. He leaned towards it, then stepped back, unsettled by the press of the water. He looked around again. He sat back, his tail curved now, arcing away from his spine. Then he did this:

He bounced back to the tree he had descended, and his rustling bustle brought the roe deer forward to where I wanted her, looking curiously. Not now, not now...

The squirrel turned right at the first big limb and ran along it, which took him more or less directly above the roe's head. She inclined her head and looked up at him. He ran on. She inclined her head the other way and looked at him. He jumped as he ran, and ran as he landed on a slender branch of a neighbouring tree. The seen-it-all-before deer went back to her browsing. The squirrel reached the second trunk, scrambled down perhaps two feet until he came to another branch. This branch was broken about eight feet out from the trunk, but not snapped off. Beyond the break it reached down towards the water and rested not in the river itself but on a rock with a steep triangular face interrupted only where the river had smoothed out a little scoop. The squirrel ran out to the break, bounced over it on to the slope of the broken branch, reached the rock, spread himself wide and head-first across its slope, and froze. Then he lapped all the water he needed from the scooped-out hollow in the middle of the rock.

There followed a movement too fast for my eye to pin down, in which he reversed his position so that he faced up the rock and his tail was snug against his spine again. Then he retraced his steps, back up the broken branch, over the break, along the branch, up the trunk, along another branch, leaped over the roe deer's turned back on to the original tree, climbed high into its canopy and vanished.

Questions.

Did he know about the broken branch?

If he did, had he used it before?

Did it come into his reckoning only when the river was too high and too turbulent to drink from the bank?

Or was this the first time he had used it?

Did he pull back from the river to weigh up other possibilities?

If so, did he see the branch and know that the rock held water?

If so, how did he know the rock held water?

Had he seen it from above?

Was the whole thing a sophisticated, premeditated manoeuvre?

Or was it a spectacular, flat-out piece of natural instinct?

Answers: I have no idea, none at all.

The doe had turned and stepped back to where I wanted her. She was beautifully shadowed and the light behind her was yellow. I raised the camera and the shutter sounded like an avalanche of rocks. Her head went up at once and she stared at me, ears forward. I took one more photograph. Still she stared. Five minutes later, neither of us had moved, so I took a third photograph.

What now? She lost interest and browsed towards the darkest edge of the clearing. I sat on until she had stepped into the shadows, and because the day required nothing more of me, I sat on another hour, during which nothing moved but the river, and I had imprinted on my mind the route-map of a red squirrel through a scrap of pinewood and riverbank.

When I processed the photographs of the roe deer, I noticed this: that the only difference between the second and third photographs – absolutely the only difference – was the position of her left ear. In five minutes, that was all she had moved. Try it some time, in a quiet and wondrously green corner of the pinewood. You'll be amazed what still-ness can turn up.

Chapter Seven

Drab, Greyish, Brindled, Grizzled

BRAERIACH IS A colossus, brutal and bitten, defended on every side but the south by a gauntlet of corries. There are ten, more or less, and depending on how you care to define 'corrie', slung in a crazed curve from south-west to south-east. In the south, there is only the lonely slog of contours where the Great Moss develops ideas above its station and thrusts a spongy arm towards the wide and steepening boulderfield of the highest plateau. Braeriach is not the highest, but in every other sense it is the mightiest upthrust of the Cairngorms, and the one which most generously rewards enthusiastic exploration. There is a lifetime's work in those corries, and an awesome expedition to link them all in a single sunwise circumnavigation. Sunwise because it is the natural order of things and because it saves the best for last – or the worst depending on how you respond to such an immense gesture of landscape as the Garbh Choire. From its furthest headwall to the Lairig Ghru (into which it thrusts the young and writhing River Dee) is two miles. From the headwall of Coire Dhondail in the south-west to the headwall of Coire Benaidh in the north-east, Braeriach stretches a three-mile plateau summit. Add its northern boulder slopes and a degree of discussion about where Braeriach begins in the south and where the Moine Mhor ends, and call it four miles from stem to stern. Summon the plateau edge which creeps up to Cairn Toul and Devil's Point and you have a mountain mass unique even by the standards of the Cairngorms.

Cairn Gorm itself and the creeping stain of development which it insinuates as far as Ben MacDui and Loch Avon – these lie east of the Lairig, and for as long as you submit to the force field of Braeriach, they feel half a world away. In all the Cairngorms massif, here is nature's sacred ground. Here too is where I have spent the headiest and most glorious, the grimmest and most fearful hours of all my days among mountains.

It did not begin well.

Gleann Einich had been heaven, glittering and warm, June sun and an easy breeze after early rain. Coire Dhondail was hell. I looked up to where my climbing companions pressed relentlessly towards the corrie's black and lowering ceiling. Couldn't they see it? Were they colour-blind to the shade of black? Why did it not terrorise their hearts as it did mine? No-one could climb through that. I had always thought that heaven was above hell? Not in the Cairngorms, it seemed. But I was young, trusting, fit and clueless. I followed on. We hit the ceiling and climbed on. I had never known such winds. Then it went dark. Then the mountain spooled that June day back through the year and dumped it somewhere in January. The wind filled with sleety snow which stung. A voice from further up the mountain pronounced that we would pitch our tents.

Here?

It was not a good night. The tent caught fire (don't ask). The fire did not improve the tent's capacity to keep out the mountain night, the wind and the snow. Mostly I remember the cold, and once, when I went outside at 2am, the most inconsolable blackness.

In the morning, the blessed, daylit, windless morning, the expedition split. Two climbed on. Two retreated. I was a retreater. I had to be home that night anyway, an excuse I brandished eagerly, but I was shaken by the nature of the mountain where I had spent the night. Another night in half a tent did not entice me. I watched the climbers climb, and the corrie walls grew vast as they dwindled upwards, atoms of movement in so much motionlessness.

I never went casually into the Cairngorms again. Far down Gleann Einich, I stopped and looked back. I was dry and growing warm again, but Braeriach was black and its sky was mobile and animated. I knew then that here was a landscape which, more than any other, I wanted to taste. When eventually I did taste it, it was instantly addictive.

I realised how far I had travelled in 25 intervening years during the Cailleach days with David Craig. I offer you his own description from *Landmarks* as we went in search of the Bodach on his rim of Coire Dhondail:

> As rain began to storm horizontally across the glen, we skirted the top of the headwall, and struggled through a torment of hummock and bog and lochan, passing amphitheatres floored with boulders like charnel pits full of old men's heads. We contoured north again along collapsing slopes strewn with clumps washed down by incessant rains, peering up at each crag, willing it to shape itself into a rough human likeness...

We failed to find a convincing Bodach. Then as the weather roused from hostility to violence we trekked the endless trek across the corrie, the same corrie where the tent caught fire, the same corrie where I fretted sleeplessly through the night; and although Dave and I found it wind-whipped and rain-sluiced and no less daunting than my young baptism of fire and other elements, I caught myself tiptoeing over one more collapsing slope and thinking: 'This is living.'

I had learned in the intervening years not to confront the mountain, or to feel confronted by it, but to co-operate with it. If you don't want to participate in the sensations offered by extremes of climate, then don't expect to tarry among extremes of landscape. But Braeriach is an extreme of landscape to which I had grown close. Its very absence of compromise is its most enlivening trait. The fact that now and again its weather has the capacity to reduce supposedly waterproof and breathable clothing to the consistency and the effectiveness of a wet bus ticket is part of the equation. So Braeriach began for me in Coire Dhondail, and when I next planted a tent there I was alone and my first fear had evolved into profound respect.

Days like the Bodach day can wear you down, heap physical exhaustion with mental misery, but only if you let yourself forget where you are, only if you relinquish your sense of purpose. My sense of purpose in the high Cairngorms is to learn their secrets. They hold different secrets from any other landscape in Scotland, and prising them free is more than one lifetime's work. But you work with what you have, with the time and the energies you are allowed. And when the mountain releases its own energies, and you happen to be in their path, you can let it all overwhelm you and wear you down, or you can try and tap in. Even a horizontal storm can work in your favour. It obviously hampers physical progress, but it can galvanise a frame of mind. I don't mean that it sends me singing and dancing along the corrie's capillary ways, but rather that it heightens a kind of spiritual awareness. It releases sensibilities and magnifies them so that you carry not rocks in your head but mountains, so that you can envisage not just the mountain burn under your feet but the whole mountain-embracing gamut of waters. This storm has gorged not just the burn you step over, but every burn, every river, every rivulet, every snowfield seepage on every corrie headwall on Braeriach. How many is that? How much water? Think of the water running off the mountain's back the way it sheets off a swan's back in a downpour. Imagine Allt Luineag urging down all the waters of the Moine Mhor, hurling them into the Eidart, the Eidart force-feeding the Feshie, the Feshie consuming a hundred Eidarts and heaping all that mountain water on the Spey; think what the Garbhh Choire looks like, the Dee a young thunderer there. Think all that, see the white water convulse and converge all across the great raised up and storm-blackened mass of the mountain.

Then marvel.

So often, that is my bottom line in the Cairngorms. You can go so far in the search for the mountain's secrets. Then one day you go looking for a pillar of rock on a mountainside of rock and it flays you with walls of water. You do not understand the natural forces at work. Their scope is utterly beyond you. But you can reach out for the sense of them, grasp what you can, and marvel.

In the midst of that old crossing of Coire Dhondail, with my nerve-ends as afire as my skin was sodden, sounds of the far-off red deer rut buffeted among the winds, broken by that louder roaring, but carrying an unmistakable note of frenzy. Were they too energised by the storm? A stag's voice, nearer than the others – somewhere below and behind – put a form of words in my mind, these words:

This was my world, the cradle of my species, shared with the wild creatures...

The word stuck in my head like a mantra, but for a moment I couldn't pin them down. I was about to ask Dave if they made any sense to him, he being a professor of creative writing between mountain exploits, when the stag roared again, and I saw an image on a page, a stag roaring and massively close, but blurred by a sodden mist. Then I remembered their source: Gavin Maxwell, tormented, as he saw it, by a curse placed on him by the poet Kathleen Raine through the portentous medium of a rowan tree:

...The days that I spent on the hill, in worse weather conditions than it is easy to visualise, gave to me a feeling of complete and utter release, of a unity with nature that I had long lacked at Camusfearna.

He wrote of one such day's deerstalking...'bloodless enough to satisfy the most squeamish'...

Suddenly, from far away, from the hidden hill-face beyond the gulf, borne thin and clear on the wind, wild and elemental, came the sound that during all the many years I have spent among the red deer of Scotland, in their aloof tempestuous territory of rock and mist, has never lost its fascination for me – the voice of the stag in rut. It begins low and throaty like a bull's roar, then hollows out to a higher, dying cadence, that seems to hold at the same time challenge, despair and frustration. I stirred to that desolate music as I stirred to the whip of wind and rain, to the ice-cold cling of my drenched clothing, to the hard ache of long unused muscles that had climbed from the infinitely distant floor of the glen below. With the water running down my neck and spine all the way to water-logged shoes, with the cold so bitter that I was conscious of my own shivering, I felt an actual buoyancy, an uplift of spirit. This was my world, the cradle of my species, shared with the wild creatures; it was the only world I wanted, and I felt I had no place at a writing desk…

…With the deer gone, I was left upon the clouded hilltop with the light going, soaked with the almost horizontal rain cutting to my ribs, and five miles to walk home in the dusk, but I was content. Here, perhaps, I was beyond the range of the rowan tree.

I have grown so familiar with the books of Gavin Maxwell over the years, that whole passages surface in my head from time to time. He may have felt he had no place at a writing desk, but I am one of many who have stirred to the possibilities of writing my own landscapes through his example. All of us who write, and most of us who read, stumble across authors from time to time who seem to be writing exclusively for our own pleasure. Maxwell had an unerring ability to put my states of mind on to the page, or to articulate perfectly ideas or philosophies which blundered in my head half-baked and ill-judged. We were so unlike in so many ways and our backgrounds were chalk and camembert (council house Dundee in my case, direct descent from the Dukes of Argyll and Northumberland in his), yet we evolved a massif of common ground, and I have often wondered how much I would have written had I not whiled away the spare time and wages of my young journalist years turning his pages and exploring his shores and rocks and rings of bright water.

As far as I know, he never wrote a word about the Cairngorms, and they will always be an east-coaster's landscape rather than that of one as thirled to the west as he was, but here was the same sentiment, the same telling word – content – nudging me across Coire Dhondail of all places where so much began for me so many years before. I have no problem with the time I spend at the writing desk (on the contrary, I love to write, and I guess that Maxwell protested too much), and as far as I know I work uncursed by poets and rowan trees, but all our lives have circumstances above which it is good to be elevated from time to time. It just doesn't happen for everyone in a horizontal storm on a black mountain.

There would come a day, then, when I carried my own tent up into that corrie, spent a tolerable enough night (there are no comfortable nights on granite boulderfields), and forged my own early morning route up through shadowed crags and out on to that higher plane where there were no shadows other than my own and the world was instantly wide and the sky curved on forever. I was drunk on space.

I walked, not along the corrie rims, but, as far as I could judge, up the very middle of that massive mountain slipway which eases up out of the Great Moss, north for Braeriach's gaunt skull.

It is an astounding place, that ramp, primarily because of how it liberates your mind. All the way out of Gleann Einich, all the way up the huge corrie walls with their amphitheatres 'floored with boulders like charnel pits full of old men's heads', the mountain comes at you in bludgeons, pile upon pile of sensations, heaped and higher-heaped shapes. Then suddenly you cross one more fractured gully, lever yourself up and the sun hits you full in the face. There is no crag left, no 'up' left, and your hands and eyes are at ground level. A tiny plant you have never seen before is in your hand, and its warmth is like a gentle electric shock.

Maxwell is in my head again...see how well he travels:

> There is, I have always found, something revital-
> ising, re-energising, in this contact between hands
> and body and the small growth of mountain
> earth.

You should be tired by the climb. Instead you spring out on to the plateau and the dark walls fall away. Their memory falls away. The glens below fall away. The idea of mountain summits falls away. You have climbed beyond all the vertical scale of Scotland. There is nothing left but breadth. You see nothing of the world but the stony incline where you walk and the sky in which your home planet floats.

I spoke a single word aloud:

'Space.'

Space. The very word sounds like itself. Space in hard white waves, blue at the edges. Space you can walk on, a sure granitic space...Somewhere in the last half-hour I must have breasted it, then kicked it apart a few moments later. I see no reason why contours should exist only on land and cheerfully chalk them on to the mountain space as I breathe it in. From where I stand, the shape of the planet makes sense, a so-wide and gently rumpled curve.

The plateau narrows to half a mile or so, like a neck atop shoulders. Beyond the neck, the great hoary skull of Am Braigh Riabhach, Braeriach. Braigh is prosaic enough, meaning 'summit'. But my old Gaelic dictionary has a poet's thesaurus stashed away against Riabhach: 'drab, greyish, brindled, grizzled'.

Chapter Eight

A Stupefying Simplicity

I WANT YOU to see this, this routine haunt of miracles, but softly, one at a time.

I want you to sit beside it, look at it, listen to it – especially listen to it – and if you have a mind, taste it. I don't care where you go, you will never see anything like it, unless you come back and sit here again. When you have looked and listened and tasted, I want you to look around and remember where you are, remember where the miracle unfolds.

No – it doesn't 'unfold' does it? It bursts. But it bursts gently, gently but irresistibly. You could no more confine its gentle energy than you could catch Niagara in a bucket.

You did well to choose today to see it, for it does not always appear as itself. Sometimes you cannot see it at all, nor hear it, and obviously in those circumstances you cannot taste it. Yet it is still where it always is! Still working miracles. Sometimes the ice seems to confine it. Sometimes, if there is a weight of snow on the ice (a far from rare occurrence hereabouts), that silences it. But it is only silent to human ears. It is not silent to itself, nor is it confined. It is always free. It is a pure source. Taste it again! Your life will know nothing purer than this.

You know the word 'elemental'? This is what it means. This is an element at its source, before you or I have had the chance to corrupt it. Nature in the raw, a primitive thing, and utterly, utterly baffling. Nan Shepherd, poet of these mountains, wrote:

> Like all profound mysteries, it is so simple that it frightens me.

It is water. Fuaran Dhé, the Wells of Dee, 4000 feet, the summit plateau of drab, greyish, brindled, grizzled Braeriach.

It wells. It springs. You look at it and you suddenly understand why wells are called wells and springs springs. It is what they do. What wells here, what springs, is the River Dee. What astounds me is that it gathers up its various wellings and springings and is at once river, a 4000-feet-high river. I want to invent something which lets me see inside the mountain. I want to X-ray its ribcage and its organs to see how this works. I want to know how the river begins. No – I can see how the river begins. I want to see how the wells begin, I want to see what urges them to well, what galvanises the springs to spring. I want to know if there is a great chamber of water. Is the mountain hollow? I want to know how the mountain inhales the juices of clouds and fills itself, and I want to understand the workings of that infallible pump which wells and springs water out on to the plateau so that it makes a river of itself at once, without benefit of gorges, confluences, lochs, tributaries. It is itself and nothing else, a stupefying simplicity.

But its welling, springing momentum is its own downfall. With all the unfettered scope of the plateau and the Great Moss at its disposal to the south, and the prospect of wide and leisured miles all the way to Glen Feshie, it chooses north-east instead, not half a leisured mile, cuts its own groove into the rim of the Garbh Choire, and jumps off.

Geronimo! Aberdeen here we come.

So I follow it as far as the rim, beyond which it becomes the Falls of Dee. Already it has forgotten how to spring and well. Instead it falls, and it has a new voice, something more baritone then all that has gone before, though with what tongues it converses deep inside the mountain before the welling and springing, I have trouble imagining.

There are days, too, when it forgets how to fall. These are the days of big winds cramming up the Lairig Ghru then bending and fanning out mightily into the yawn of the Garbh Choire, pouring down the mountain's open throat, and so nonchalantly flipping the Falls back up head over their own heels and drenching their own riverbanks in watery perpetual motion that you watch with your breath held. And yes, you marvel.

But I'm not ready for the Garbh Choire yet. I'm still besotted by the well-springing, still high on the adrenaline of the plateau, still possessing the drab, greyish, brindled, grizzled sensations of the mountaintop. It is an extraordinary place to be on a plateau between two precipices with almost nothing that is higher than the place where you stand, with a vast spreadeagling of Highlands to the south and west and north (not east – there glowers Ben MacDui soiled by the excesses of Cairngorm), and at your feet the rustling, gurgling, grunting, whispering of the Dee changing worlds, the underworld for the overworld.

I have been cold here beyond any sense of cold I thought it was possible to feel. It is the work of the wind, that cold, and it is as lethal as avalanches, and – as Seton Gordon never tired of pointing out – as Arctic as Spitzbergen. But I have been warm here too, one August day when the planet stood on its own head and it was cool on Speyside, clouded below the belt of corries to which Braeriach hitches the bouldered pleats of its skirts, and warm and still on the plateau where the sun held sway for fifteen hours. I am a stranger to the mountains in summer, but I make my exception to my own rule for this patch of the Cairngorms plateau, because summer here is unlike other definitions of summers in lesser landscapes. It is a brief and traumatic season, when grass and bud and leaf rush out and you learn to expect the unexpected.

Look there: in the first yard of that welling of water, there is a flurry of activity not water. Look. Wings! Something is bathing there. It rises on its tail and turns, so that its white front is in the sunlight. A dipper! The highest bird bath in Scotland. He stands for a moment, shakes himself free of a tiny shower of drops, then spreads his wings on the ground like a back garden blackbird sunning himself. Why is he here? The mountain is awash with hill burns and pools, gravelly shallows and (one would imagine) richer feeding than this. Five years before I had found one on the frozen shore of Loch Coire an Lochain at 3300 feet in April and thought I had made a rare discovery. Now this. Dipper flight is enslaved to watercourses, and there are none between Loch Coire an Lochain and the Wells of Dee, so not the same bird then. But there are watery tendrils of Coire nan Clach (the casually named Stony Corrie) or Coire Bogha-Cloiche which reach almost as high as the Wells, and a dipper might adventure up one of these on a warm day that made high-flying effortless. It all suggests at the very least a sophisticated knowledge of mountain weather and summit conditions, and of course the knowledge that the highest birdbath in Scotland was there.

But this is more properly ptarmigan country, and dotterel country, and snow bunting country (although I have never seen one on Braeriach, a curious omission on my part), the tribes of Arctic stoics. Seton Gordon narrates an extraordinary detail, from July, 1923:

> At just 3925 feet above sea level – I mention the height because one rarely finds ptarmigan nesting at so great an altitude – a ptarmigan flew on white wings from her shallow nest containing three eggs. These eggs were unusual in shape, for they were long, thin and rather pointed. An interesting sequel was the finding of the nest of the same bird with similar curiously shaped eggs in the summer of 1924 within a hundred yards of the same spot.

It is part of an extraordinary account of the events of that summer. Snow had fallen well into June, and the great man encountered the Braeriach plateau on 3 July with 'all the appearance of midwinter'. There was an iceberg on Loch Coire an Lochain and he guessed it would have been frozen across until mid-June. At the Wells of Dee,

> the grass was brown, and lay close-pressed upon the ground as though a mountain torrent had passed over it. Not a bud showed upon the innumerable plants of the dwarf willow and the rosettes of the cushion pink were brown and apparently lifeless.

As for the Wells of Dee themselves,

one could walk above the wells yet be unaware of their existence.

Then after nine days of warm weather, Seton Gordon returned and found the place under enchantment.

> ...an almost unbelievable change had been wrought on the face of the earth...

There was new grass two or three inches long, the dwarf willow was in full leaf and the pinks had leafed and budded. But...

> Summer had come with a rush to the Cairngorms, but a full month of precious warmth had been lost to the hills, and summer that year lasted no more than a fortnight, for on the 26th July a bitter north-west wind with driving snow swept the plateau of the Wells...

Such is the nature of high summer. I wonder what colour the mountain hares were that year, for protracted winters often inhibit the change of their coats from white to summer brown, and in a two-week summer, it hardly seems worth the trouble.

My preference is always autumn, which mostly means winter in the Cairngorms. October reliably brings the first snows which linger (although snow on the plateau is a twelve-month phenomenon: seasoned Cairngorms trekkers, whatever their motives, have all been snowed on in every month of the year). The mountain has already lost its brief green sheen, and even its shades of September fire have dulled to an ochreous orange. Then the snow, then the hard frosts, then the sun, and how the mountain air electrifies! The mountain turns its darkest red in October, the Monadh Ruadh of the Gaelic tongue which named them Red Mountains, and any sunset catching the highest curving rim of snow puts a pinkish swathe above that dark red, and it looks as if the mountain is slowly draining the colour from the snow, the way it imbibes water so that the Dee might well and spring.

The passage of geese south above the great troughs of the Cairngorms is a feature of the autumn mountain, Arctic voices layered levelly on the air, a second plateau of sound. I have seen them at (an uncalculated guess devoid of all useful scale) about 7000 feet so that the sound of them fell on a stupendous mountain silence like flakes of silver confetti, or a light snow of sounds, something as flimsy as that. But I have also seen them flying up Gleann Einich well below the level of the plateau so that they had to climb to hurdle the headwall of Coire Odhar at the southern end of the glen, and trying (a more calculated guess based on the northward passage of much higher clouds) to stay under a band of contrary winds.

The sound of wild geese overhead was the first voice of nature which ever made an impression on me, as a child in Dundee where geese on the Tay are as integral a part of existence there as sea winds and dropped 't's in the stree's. So as a child I grew up thinking that geese were somehow part of Dundee's personal property, something fine that went with the territory. They still have that power, wherever I encounter them, to reconvene my first awakening awareness of nature amid frosted and still gaslit streets. They would wake me in the night, clattering low overhead for

Invergowrie Bay after staying late in the fields to feed under the moon, so they wove their way into young dreams and they orchestrated their own spectacle. So when (over years, of course) I progressed from the fields above the house to the Sidlaw Hills (a sure northwards progress) then to the Angus Glens and then to the Cairngorms (always the ultimate northern horizon for one schooled in Dundee's hill-going tradition) and found geese there, it was like being born again. At childhood's sea level they were always high and wildly aloof. But the first time I climbed on to the Braeriach plateau and heard them, having climbed higher than I had ever climbed before, and still they were high and wildly aloof and cutting the sky with scissored flights, something new stirred in me. I was never able to define it, but it felt sure and somehow honourable because I had found in this mightiest of all my native landscapes a common bond with the first of all my landscapes. It was as if my life's path had been reinforced for me, as if nature's role in my life had suddenly been elevated to new heights. So it is a bright torch I carry for the wild geese of Braeriach and Tayside.

And once, too, from a random seat high on the Beanaidh Bheag burn which drains Coire Beanaidh, northmost of the mountain's corries, I saw a skein of twelve whooper swans flying up Gleann Einich, and not 500 feet above the river. As I watched from my higher perch, the sun was on their backs and the topsides of their wings. The clarity of the Cairngorms air is always conducive to the transport of sound, and their voices carried more than a mile to where I sat.

I have watched a lot of swans over many years now. Their way of life is among my favourite themes as a writer, and they have repaid many times my countless hours of patient study. Now I sensed at once the disconcertion in their flight long before its source became apparent. Their soft contact calls became the louder and discordant bells of alarm, and I saw them break from their flightpath, wheel into the wind on stiffened wings and put down on a small loch west of the river. There they cruised restlessly, with their necks tall and their voices raised, and some fluke of the rocks above the loch bounced an echo of their voices across the glen.

I puzzled over the spectacle. In the first place it is not a particularly typical whooper swan migration route. Their passage to Scotland from Iceland is normally by way of the coasts, then moving inland to favourite haunts by way of east-west glens and firths. And given that one such haunt – the Insh Marshes – was only a handful of miles to the west, what were they doing here, heading deep into the mountains, and in some distress? Besides, whoopers normally *fly* in the face of adversity, not put down on water. Unless...I ran through a shortlist of 'unlesses'...unless the source of their distress was already in the air.

I scanned skies and the glen's airspace and found a golden eagle nudging the contours a thousand feet above the loch, a young bird with vivid white wing patches, lazy on the air, but hardly threat enough to crash-land a dozen swans. Eagles have been known to strike down a goose in flight and finish it off on the ground, but an adult whooper is a huge bird, the male as big as any female eagle, and much heavier. Then I found a second eagle, and then a third, high over a shoulder of Sgoran Dubh Mor, and doubtless having their eagle-eyed attention drawn to the white splash and the raised voices of the swans. The three birds would be a family group, and if the swans were already troubled by being off-course and in the wrong glen, the sight of three eagles close together and above them might just explain the why and the wherefore of what I had seen.

The eagles drifted on and curved west above the Sgoran crags, but the swans sat on. I wondered how long they might sit. I had perhaps three hours of daylight left, and the Gleann Einich track is no hardship in the dark. It was a reasonable enough afternoon for sitting, so I just sat. Now and again I looked behind and above at the darkening mass of the mountains, or across the Lairig at Lurcher's Crag, one of the Cairngorms' few angular shapes. I drank burn water and crunched a couple of biscuits, scribbled a bit, felt the wind loosen its hold on the day, but mostly I just sat and watched the distant swans. Their voices calmed, but they did not visibly relax, nor did they fly on. As the light in the glen began to fade, their whiteness became the brightest shade I could see, and still they sat on the water, and still they held their necks high and muttered out loud.

I gave in. I put the last hour of useable light to work toiling down the vast bouldery flank of Braeriach, pausing often to look back and up, marking my snail-sized progress down the mountain because I like to remind myself of my absence of size in the scale of the Cairngorms. It makes you plant your feet carefully. I reached the track, waved at the mountain, turned and waved at the unseen swans, and walked on into the gloom of the pinewoods, and as I walked my path was lit by the white glow of swans, and the sound of their voices in my head. My tent was pitched at the end of the track, and it was still dark when I retraced the evening's steps next morning. I came in quietly on the swans' loch as the sun rose, but it was devoid of swans. They had gone in the dusk or the dark or the dawn.

So it is more than water which flows from the Wells of Dee. It is a fountainhead for wildness, too. It is nature's place, more absolutely than any other place I know. It is nature's forces which hold sway, a turbulent, bullying regime which thrives undiminished because it deals only in extremes. There are no compromises, and those of us who linger there do so briefly, and with the wariness of the trespasser. Sooner or later, we know that forces will be mustered with which we are incapable of co-existing. This is not our place. It is a place for primitive things – inch-high trees, ptarmigan with elongated eggs, dotterel and snow bunting and mountain hare, snow and wind and water. Water so profoundly mysterious it frightens.

Among the crazed and chilling minds of those who see not nature in the high Cairngorms but an exploitable 'resource', there have been such Satanic contributions over the years as proposals to put a road through the Lairig Ghru, ski-tows up into the Garbh Choire, and from there up on to the plateau of Braeriach. The kind of outrage and contempt I feel for such notions is matched only by the shame I feel because they have emerged from others of the same species as me. If the funicular railway is ever built on Cairn Gorm, and if it ever attracts the kind of visitor numbers its backers prophesied, then the plateaux of Cairn Gorm and Ben MacDui will not hold them. Eyes will turn elsewhere, and they will see this place. That is why I wanted you to see this, this routine haunt of miracles, but softly, one at a time. So that you know what is at risk.

Chapter Nine

A Wasteland with no Half Measures

AM MOINE MHOR, the Great Moss, is not easy to define, neither on the map nor on the ground. Maps point with some hesitation and in their smallest type to somewhere between the south of Gleann Einich and north-east of Coire Garbhlach. Do they mean the single square mile of scattered headwaters of a burn called Caochan Dubh which in turn feeds into the River Eidart, that single square mile where the name usually crops up? Or – if you are to believe your own eyes and the nature of the ground north, west and south of those same headwaters and a tapering wedge as far east as Loch nan Stuirteag – did those who named the place (and who never had to worry about placements on maps because of the maps they carried in their heads) have in mind a fist-ful of square miles?

I incline towards the latter proposition. The 'Moss' in question is not the one which greens an ageing dyke but the one which embodies notions of elevated space, unchancy underfoot, a place bare from peat workings, and where it is not bare it is mostly wet, awkward in cloud, a repository for botanical curios, and by and large bereft of all other saving graces, a wasteland, and – because it is in the high Cairngorms – a wasteland with no half measures.

Say, for the sake of ordering that chaos of ill-definition, you cramponed eagerly up the solid snow of Coire

Garbhlach's narrow and tucked-away headwall, and having burst open its little cornice and peered over the top, blinking in sunlight (with which the narrow twists of the corrie are sparing), you stop and stare. Almost as far as you can see is a floundering morass of undulation. 'Almost' because in the far east of the land there is the reliable upheaval of Cairn Toul, blunt and conning-tower-ish on the skyline. But there is not much else to focus on.

You wander out into this new space for half a mile or so, relishing its breadth, the antithesis in all the Cairngorms' landforms of the one you left behind in the corrie which was not so much a corrie as a kind of crooked Lairig Ghru going nowhere. You look north to Carn Bàn Mór, a low swelling of the Moss, nothing more, certainly not a Big White Cairn. But then it was not named from here, it was named from down on the Feshie side of the hill, where a turgid series of false summits toils up to it from Carn Bàn Beag, the wee one, and from there it amounts to a skyline of a kind. The Great Moss, on the other hand, is invisible from down there, and shapeless when you stand in its midst, so give it a vagueness in small type and no-one can say you're wrong.

You walk the gentle mile to the Carn, and find that the Moss, or something indistinguishable from it in terms of terrain, thrusts out another tapering wedge, north this time, to Sgòr Gaoith, and close enough to the Cailleach on her corrie wall to shake a passing fist at. You follow the wall back looking for the Moine Mhor's one known address. You found it that day with David Craig, Fuaran Diotach, which Seton Gordon memorably translates as 'Luncheon Springs'. It was not finding the spring which was remarkable here, but finding a shieling wall thoughtfully tacked on to a rock outcrop, frontless and roofless, but its size and shape clear enough. Who on earth built it, and why? Surely it had a story. Surely Seton Gordon would know it, but his seminal Cairngorms work mentions it but once:

> Beside Fuaran Diotach (the Luncheon Springs) my companion and I lunched, at the edge of the snowfield.

End of story, my crest fallen. Could it be that this was the great man's solitary sojourn here, and the old stones were under the snow? Did he pass up the opportunity to narrate one more of those Cairngorms legend he so loved because he was sitting on it?

Whatever he missed, it was surely an unsung chapter of the Cailleach's story, and my best guess is that it was something like this:

When the Cailleach was in her prime, and more mobile by far than she is today, she was a formidable adversary for the Bodach, who suffered grievously at her hands. Her aim at the rock throwing was better than his, so he suffered more wounds than she, and her tongue was sharper than his so her barbs and insults cut deeper.

One spring when the shieling folk came up the lochside with their beasts and he began snarling down at them (and at that the Cailleach would sing their praises and urge them to resist the Bodach's taunts – anything to further infuriate him), he suddenly realised that his son was among them. His son was both handsome and unusually strong, and the Bodach was not short of cunning. In the night he conceived a plan.

The following morning, he had changed his tune towards the shieling folk, apologising for his wrath, and wishing them a prosperous summer, and he would see to it that they would not be inconvenienced in any way. At that – and this was the reliable part of his plan – the Cailleach turned against them, lashed them with her screeched insults, peppered their roofs with unerring accuracy. The Bodach let this go on for a couple of days, then summoned his son and told him this:

'Do you think you could topple the old hag from her perch up there on the cliff, my son? You with your great strength and all that I have taught you about stealth and cunning?'

'I'll do whatever you ask, Father, of course, but how am I to get close without her seeing me and smashing me to pieces with one of her rocks?'

'I have thought about that. I can provide a shelter of rocks for you, close to the foul-mouthed battleaxe, and you shall climb up to it under the cover of darkness. At first light, you rush out and topple her into the loch! Will you do it, son?'

'Yes, Father. If that's what you want.'

So the Bodach embarked on a frenzy of rock throwing, but instead of aiming for the Cailleach, he aimed a little to the north of her where the spring rises above the corrie headwall. The Cailleach mocked his poor aim, told him in her most hideous voice that he had grown old and feeble.

But the rocks rained down well into the dusk, and even in the dark, and in her determined scoffing and taunting and laughing the Cailleach failed to notice that as the rocks landed they arranged themselves into a low and curving wall which leaned against a rock buttress, and left just enough room for someone to creep in undetected.

A little after midnight, the Bodach's son crept out from the shieling, climbed the south wall of Coire Odhar, then taking care never to break the skyline or loosen so much as a single stone, he moved silently round the rim of the corrie, and guided by the sound of the springs, he found the shelter and slipped inside. He lay down and waited for dawn.

He was uneasy about the task his father had set him, and began to wonder if the old hag was just as bad as his father had painted her. It seemed to him, and to the other shieling folk who had to thole their outbursts, that one was as bad as the other, and that both were worse than they needed to be. He wrestled with the idea for hours, until eventually he fell asleep, and did not wake up until long after sunrise. By then, of course, the Cailleach had seen the stone wall, peered inside, and found the sleeping figure...

...The Bodach was enraged. It was midday, and still the Cailleach haunted her cliff top. Why was she not drowned in the loch by now? Why had his son failed him? He could hardly go and investigate. The hag would see him before he had moved a yard! So he took on the guise of a stag and browsed his way across the Moine Mhor, drifted round the corrie headwall until he stood above the springs and looked down. There was his son outside the stone shelter, eating lunch with the Cailleach, and obviously getting on very well indeed with her. What treachery was this!

'What a handsome stag!' said the Cailleach.

The young man laughed, looked directly at the stag and said:

'Father! Take off that ridiculous disguise and come down here!'

So the stag became the Bodach again to the astonishment of the Cailleach who had not seen through the disguise. The Bodach was equally astonished that his son had seen through it.

'Father, it was a shameful thing you asked of me. Did you think I would not recognise my own mother, even after all these years? I know you both nurse old grievances, but I am here to tell you both that this must stop. The Eagle of the Mountains has sent me. She is ashamed of both of you. If you cannot co-exist peaceably, then you will do so in silence and as pillars of stone.

The Cailleach and the Bodach looked at each other with a great and ancient loathing. In the same instant, they said: 'Never!'

The young man stood up from the lunch where it still lay spread out on a rock by the springs, and spread his arms wide, with his palms facing down. At once he had assumed the shape of a great golden eagle. The bird circled the corrie twice, and a black hood of storm cloud rose over the Moine Mhor and boiled down into the corrie.

An hour later the wind shifted, the cloud dispersed, and Bodach and Cailleach were mute and stiff as stone facing each other across the sunlit flanks of the corrie. On the rock of Fuaran Diotach, a pair of grey crows worked over the last of the lunch. From that day, the place was known as the Luncheon Springs.

South of Coire Odhar, the Great Moss begins to fracture into tiny lochans, scraps of burns, a place as much of water as land. Loch nan Cnapan, the Loch of the Knolls (which is fair enough if a touch prosaic) is the centrepiece of it all, and its burn gathers in much of that square mile of ooze and drives it lemming-like for the headwall, where it leaps crazily down a string of waterfalls into Loch Einich.

You can stand on a slope of one of Loch nan Cnapan's many surrounding cnapan a little to the south of the loch and see two hill burns rise, perhaps fifty yards apart. One flows north into the loch, becomes waterfall, then Loch Einich, then Am Beanaidh, then it meets the Luineag at Coylumbridge and becomes the Druie, then reaches the Spey at Aviemore. The other burn, however, flows south, feeds into the Eidart, becomes the Feshie, then begins the long haul west then north to join the Spey north of Loch Insh. It just seems a lot of trouble to go to.

For the first time since you stepped up on to the Great Moss out of Coire Garbhlach, you begin to feel below something rather than on top of everything. East of Loch nan Cnapan, and certainly north-east of it, the land begins to change, to tilt and convulse. The Moss is slipping away from you, broken up and bullied into submission by the climbing thrusts of a higher order of plateau lands. Braeriach heaps massively, and it is here I think that it is at its most impressive, because psychologically you have felt all the way across the Moss that you were so *high* and suddenly it throws a monstrous thousand-foot ramp at you, reinforcing (as if it was necessary) the scope of the landscapes in which you stand.

Every now and again, crossing the Moine Mhor, I resist the temptation to toil up that ramp to the promised land beyond, and climb instead out of the Moss to the deep quiet of Loch nan Stuirteag. It lies on a small snowy plateau of its own, and seems to suffer from all the winds on earth. But it is also an island, neither obviously part of the Moss nor of the mountain mass behind. I love these places of landscape tension, where, regardless of which way you go, you commit yourself at once to a different world from the one you have just left. The Moss is at your back. The most powerful mountain mass in the Cairngorms – and therefore in all the

Highlands – rears like a breaking wave, unfurling headwalls from Braeriach to Devil's Point. But there is another option more in keeping with the spirit of the long day's trek. It is to follow the Allt Clais an t-Sabhail down into the widening curve of Glen Geusachan, the Glen of the Pines, a high-walled counterpoint to Coire Garbhlach. Glen Geusachan is home to one of the most pointless ironies of the Cairngorms, for in the Glen of the Pines Trees, there lives not a single pine. Instead, there are tree ghosts, stumps and roots, head-stones which commemorate the forest which was. It is a recurrent theme of the Cairngorms, the waning of its tree cover. Seton Gordon recorded three relics at 2300 feet here, and at 2400 in nearby Glen Luibeg. That is the nature of the place which was, a massif rearing from a forest which half-clothed its great girth. Now, only at Craig Fhiaclach on the edge of Rothiemurchus does the natural treeline nudge fleetingly through the 2000 feet contour.

Yet it had been shown – notably by the RSPB in Abernethy – how the pinewoods can be rejuvenated. And Rothiemurchus's more benevolent estate management than is the norm in the Cairngorms has saved and nurtured good tracts of pinewoods. There is a reawakening of interest in the old pine forest, a new awareness of its worth. But the best of intentions so often succumb to the mire of committees, bureaucracies, vested interests and political obstruction. I commend to all who consider themselves to be champions of the Cairngorms and their pinewoods, the little story called *The Man Who Planted Trees* by Jean Giono. It is a story, but it crystallises the merits of direct action in conservation's cause. If we want the pines of Glen Geusachan to flourish again, and find their own altitude, we must find a way of putting them there. I do not mean holding multi-party talks to seek the consensus, the relentless mind-numbing quest for compromise. I mean putting trees in the ground. Then find a way of keeping too many deer (the servants of yet more vested interests) away from the trees.

Always, in the Cairngorms, for all their wildness, all their natural majesty, you keep stumbling up against forces of oppression ranged against the natural order. Their purpose is always the same – self-interest. Their overriding characteristics are always the same – greed, narrow-mindedness, indifference.

The great east-west trek from Coire Garbhlach by way of the Moine Mhor to Glen Geusachan is a classical mountain journey by any standards, its landscapes primitive, diverse, confining, liberating. Yet it begins in Glen Feshie, whose recent history has been a byword for the worst kind of estate management; its decrepit pinewoods and mountain roads crudely bulldozed far out on to the Great Moss are its hallmarks. It has new owners who profess good intentions. We wait and wonder. They are not the first. The day's journey crossed into Mar Lodge estate, for which all the above also apply. The new owner is the National Trust for Scotland, no-one's idea of a godsend based on their track record of managing other mountains. The journey descends by way of Glen Geusachan. How long before its pines grow green again? How long before a wolf cries into its open gape from Clais a'Mhadaidh? The way it looks at the moment, there is as much likelihood of the one as the other.

You move slowly through Glen Geusachan, the way you move slowly through a graveyard or the site of an old battlefield. The Glen is both. Nature fought here and lost. Its unburied dead lie all around.

The glen imposes something as you walk. The deeper you

descend into its chasm, the more profound the imposition. By the time you reach the point of its huge right-angle (you are reminded once more: a thing as much of space as of mountainsides), the walls have begun to rear and lean. You are grateful, if you walk alone here, for the conversable company of the river and its many tributaries; the stillness which layers all but the water is the stillness of the mortuary. The temptation is strong to turn and run and climb back to the open-palmed pleasures of airy Loch nan Stuirteag.

But I sat for a while by the banks of the river, and spilled a little of its water into the hip flask (a good mountain water liberates all manner of energies, subtleties of taste and flavour in an equally good single malt whisky – I carry no other kind), the better to try and articulate what it was I felt about the place. What was the imposition I felt? Why did I feel it here, and not, for example, in Coire Garbhlach? The tree-ghosts were obviously part of what I felt, possessed of their own contagious melancholy, and I had brushed up against enough of them on the way down the glen to catch its most virulent strain. But there was more to it than that.

There are, in my own experience of a lifetime wandering the Highlands, landscapes I like, landscapes I love, and a tiny handful of landscapes which have got under my skin. The Cairngorms come into that third category, a state of affairs which suggests to me that I am more aware of the nuances of this landscape than I am of most others. It is easier to come back to the Cairngorms and tune in than it is in, say, Sutherland. So when, after four days of re-acclimatising to the Cairngorms' extraordinary demands of scope and scale and uniqueness, I undertake a long trek from Feshie to Dee by way of the Great Moss, I feel acutely alive in these surroundings. I can justify – to myself at least – the idea that

I have grown closer to this place, that I can hear its voice more clearly.

A landscape with a voice?

I think so, yes. Clearly not a spoken language of words, but a way of communicating to all ears willing to take the time and trouble to acclimatise, tune in, and listen. I think too that that was what I sensed when I felt the imposing something – mood, atmosphere, ambience which infiltrated the highest slopes of the glen and settled ever more heavily as I walked deeper in. It was the landscape's voice, and what it articulated was a cry for help.

An absurd fantasy?

Elitist egotism?

Sentimental gibberish?

They are familiar charges. They come from those whose only forays on to the high plateaux involve the Cairn Gorm chairlift. Or those who cannot contemplate a five-mile walk-in through pinewoods without a mountain bike. Or those who have never climbed in the Cairngorms alone.

You cannot come close to nature in the mountains unless you are willing to be alone from time to time. You cannot hear the voice of the landscape if you are immersed in conversation or if you are attending to or dependent on the presence of companions. The camaraderie of people among mountains is a great thing, and not to be minimised or belittled, but it is not the be all and end all of human experience among mountains. Travelling alone assists perceptions of mountains which are beyond the reach of mob-handed expeditions. One of those perceptions is the idea of a landscape voice. Before you scoff, go alone, listen out for the great silences, and hear how they speak, and what they have to say.

You would not turn a deaf ear to a fellow mountaineer's cry for help. How much more important then that you offer the same courtesy to the mountain itself?

The Geusachan writhes east to swell the Dee under the great Lairig Ghru milestone of Devil's Point. I kept its turbulent company, then climbed and crossed wearily under Carn a' Mhaim for Glen Luibeg, Derry Lodge, and the long road home. It is a curiosity of my own Cairngorms years that although this was my very first portal into the massif, mildly traumatised by my first crossing of Jock's Road from Glen Clova, I eventually gravitated through some quite unidentifiable instinct to the Speyside portals, and now I think of Luibeg and Derry – perhaps uncharitably – as the way out. So they are reluctant, lingering places as often as not, excuse for one last camp, perhaps, when I should really have been gone 24 hours before.

So I cross the Moine Mhor from west to east. The great Lairigs, when I trouble them at all, (I subscribe to Nan Shepherd's endorsement of the Pools of Dee that 'I can conceive of no good reason for trudging through the oppressive Lairig Ghru, except to see them'), I tackle from the north. And walking south into the mountain clasp out the Gleann Einich track is the most natural process imaginable, this creature in his natural habitat.

Preferences among mountains are the most unjustifiably subjective of all. How *can* one mountain be better than another? Even more unjustifiable, given the store I set in the principle of the Cairngorms as a single mountain, is my preference for the landscapes west of the Lairig Ghru to the thundering heartbeat shapes east of it. It comes down to states of mind. My state of mind is easier by far on the Braeriach of it all than on the Cairn Gorm and Ben MacDui of it all, or rather, than what Cairn Gorm and Ben MacDui have become.

A crowded mountain is my idea of hell.

The wedding of tourism and mountains is a marriage made in hell.

So I walk my lofty portions of heaven-on-earth where solitude is still an option, and silence always a possibility. It was far out on the Great Moss, during the Cailleach Days, that David Craig and I encountered what we both agreed was the most profound and total silence of all our mountaineering years. I wrote it in an earlier book, *Among Mountains*, Dave in his *Landmarks*, but then, a year later, he told me he had made a poem of the moment. The copy he subsequently sent me, entitled *The Height of the Great Moss*, is inscribed 'for Jim, who was there'. So with his blessing (and my own blessing on his sublime monument to that defining soundlessness) this is it:

> That scalp of hoar is permanent on Cairn Toul
> Whether the weather on the Moine Mhor
> Is blowing fine or foul.
> The blade of the glacier dozing over
> Laid bare that stony flay.
> Its skull of granite weathered old-man-grey
> Before the ptarmigan flew in from Jutland,
> Even before the pine.
>
> It is the colour of a silenced brain
> Bloodless and motionless as the coffined dead.
> It is the grizzled head
> Of an old peasant who will not be moved
> Even by civil war,

Who is bothered not at all
What politicians and banks are fighting for.

I have breathed this air before:
On Burrival midway down the western islands,
Little square belvedere above the waters,
Where crofters cleared from Sollas
Wintered along Loch Eport, passed on south
And left it to its silence;
On Morvern in the second year of war
Where I laid fenceposts up the summit slope
In V's for Victory,
Paused to let in the stillness of the moor,
And heard a single Heinkel grunt and snore,
Black as a condor in the summer sky.

The Great Moss lours above them all,
Spreading its blanket for a giant's bed.
Here I will lay my own expiring head
Only in fantasy
When life dissolves in ideal resignation
And dreams of dying as it ought to be –
No filth, no struggle, only embarkation
Onto the inland sea.

Chapter Ten

High and Lonely

One was reluctant to leave the high tops on an evening such as this. In the immense silences of these wild corries and dark rocks, the spirit of the high and lonely places revealed herself so that one felt the serene and benign influence that has from time to time caused men to leave the society of their fellows and live on some remote surf-drenched isle – as St Cuthbert did on Farne – there to steep themselves in those spiritual influences that are hard to receive in the crowded hours of human life.

Seton Gordon
The Cairngorm Hills of Scotland

WHEN I FIRST wrote about the Cairngorms in any depth, it was with these words as my *cri de coeur*. They provided me with a title for that book – *A High and Lonely Place* – and a supreme irony to harness to the mountain's defence. For Seton Gordon had written these words in tribute to Cairn Gorm itself, after a day out on Lurcher's Crag, which, with Lurcher's Gully to the north was to become the great symbolic battleground between Cairn Gorm's ski-ing expansionists and the dug-in heels of conservation.

I am old enough, and my Cairngorms wanderings began

young enough for me to remember Coylumbridge before the ski road, the northern corries of Cairn Gorm as unimpaired as Braeriach's are today. When Seton Gordon wrote, Cairn Gorm was as primitive as the rest of the massif, its northern corries rarely visited, Aviemore was a drab and mostly snowy blur on the A9, and Santa Claus still lived in Greenland.

What has happened since ski-ing moved in is a barely credible transformation of the mountain, beauty made beast. The only reluctance I feel there now is to go anywhere near the place. I have stood once on the summit of Cairn Gorm and I can think of no reason to go back, and to pursue Seton Gordon's sentiments further, there are no silences, immense or otherwise, the corries are not wild, the rocks are lurid with litter, and the spirit of the high and lonely places resides elsewhere. There is no serene and benign influence – it is utterly extinct on Cairn Gorm – and the crowded hours of human life have moved in.

The path from the top car park on Cairn Gorm to the foot of the Fiacaill Ridge creeps along under Coire an t-Sneachda, Corrie of the Snows, and why that one should be singled out as worthy of snowy distinction is not obvious so long after it was named. All these northern corries hold snow deep into the spring, and Corrie an t-Sneachda's distinction is not that it holds more snow than the others but that it boasts a high and unseen upper chamber, a south-westward lurch like the toe of a boot stubbed into the flanks of the Fiacaill Ridge. Seton Gordon wrote of that corner of Cairn Gorm after two weeks of unbroken snowfall, the snow 'several yards deep' in Coire an Lochain, and...

> Coire an t-Sneachda is still in mist, but the precipitous jagged ridge between it and Coire an Lochain might well be a shoulder of Everest itself.

The Cairngorms can do that. When extremes of landform and climate coincide they can elevate their own grandeur into new illusory heights, breadths, depths. The Fiacail Ridge is the last civilised route on to the Cairn Gorm plateau, protected only by its own awkward and unbalancing rocky heights. It is simple terrain for a rock climber, quite challenging for a mere scrambler like me, and out of bounds for walkers who like to keep their hands in their pockets. Ridge-climbing is not a fundamental demand made on Cairngorms explorers. Rather you have to seek out the ridges if you crave them. I don't crave them. I can't see the point of looking for ridges in a plateau landscape, of clinging to capillary edges when what the Cairngorms are all about is grand gestures, acres-wide summits, breadth, space of all things. But I was shown the Fiacaill Ridge once by my friend and fellow Cairngorms aficionado, Cameron McNeish, admired his well balanced way with the high rocks, and (a little less balanced and a little more unsure of myself, it must be said) I have borrowed it twice since then on explorations of my own. I think I won't use it again. The second time, the clamour of people on the Cairngorm plateau, the total lack of concern for where they were, the mess and the pollution of their noise, I found unforgivable. The Chairlift Company is just as culpable as the summit revellers, for it pours them on to the plateau all summer long when its sole activity is to make money. It is the crudest exploitation of nature imaginable. The numbers and the behaviour of people on the Cairn Gorm plateau that day actually frightened me. I bolted for Ben MacDui, the head-long descent into the Lairig Ghru and the blessed enfolding of the Garbh Choire.

But between first and last ascent of the Fiacaill Ridge there was a climb which launched a two-day trawl of pure September gold through that tumultuous land between the Lairig Ghru and the Lairig an Laoigh. There was the famil-iar sense of changing worlds where the ridge is bolted on to the plateau at Cairn Lochan, the suddenly easy going of the terrain, the sudden scope of the sky which curves below you in every direction so that you may as well be walking on a cloud. Sometimes September in the Highlands pro-duces a clarity in the air and a yellow-gold quality of light unknown in other months. It has the atmosphere of a lull in nature. It says summer is done, irretrievable, but autumn is not dressed yet, not ready for its grand entrance. So here is a circumstance to tide you over until the new season is fin-ished. That kind of September is weather for the Gods, so heartstopping to be out in that you feel as if you are tres-passing on nature at rest. The Cairngorms – or Skye perhaps – at such a moment is absolutely the best of every-thing.

The plateau wind was a gentle westerly. I let it nudge me towards the Feith Buidhe where I dawdled over the dark silk of Loch Avon sunk deep in its trench. I decided there and then that the expedition should revise itself to include a circumnavigation of the loch. Whim had a lot to do with the decision. I fixed in my mind an idea of where I stood, a lit-tle distance away from Hell's Lum (the best place to be – a little distance away from it) and how I might look to some-one scanning these precipices from far down the loch. That night, if the weather held, I could sit outside my own tent and look at myself as I stood hours before, bonding the day's journey into the landscape. I sauntered off to Ben MacDui, the plateau scoured by a wide (and ever widening) trench of a path, many of whose trekkers seem obsessed with building cairns, presumably to mark the line in bad weather. It is a regrettable obsession, imposing the ways of the garden centre on the wilderness. Cameron McNeish and I once kicked over twenty-something cairns here in the space of about 300 yards. Cairn demolishing has always seemed a healthier obsession than cairn building.

These hills grow quiet in late September. For an hour at the bare, bouldery summit of Ben MacDui ('Ben Mac Dhui', wrote Seton Gordon, 'is in Gaelic Beinn MacDhuibh, which in older Gaelic means "Hill of the sons of Duff"'.), I had only the wind for company, and a view which was limited only by the capacity of my eyes to look at it. Even at this distance, Ben Nevis stamped its brute mass on that infinity of mountains between here and the Atlantic. So hard-edge and limitless were the receding westward ranks of peaks and ridges that I dug out the glasses and went looking for Seton Gordon's phantom mountains. For on a day of exceptional visibility on Ben MacDui, he had written:

> In line with the Wells of Dee, at an immense distance, two tapering cones, of a faint ethereal blue, rose on the far horizon. These tops seemed a full hundred miles away. A compass bearing showed them to be on the line of the Coolin Hills of the Isle of Skye, but it has never been proved that these hills can be seen from the Cairngorms. It is possible they were the heights of Kintail, but the shape was very like that of Sgurr nan Gillean

of the Coolin peaks. On the north-westerly horizon An Teallach, also on the western seaboard,
seemed but a stone's throw away in comparison.

I found what I took to be Kintail, and there was no mistaking An Teallach, but I found no pair of ethereal cones. The
idea of seeing Skye from the Cairngorms so charmed me
that a few days later, I did some measuring with a map and
piece of string. From Ben MacDui to Sgurr nan Gillean,
about 105 miles; from Ben MacDui to An Teallach, about 85;
from Ben MacDui to Sgur Fhuaran of Kintail only 60 miles.
So if An Teallach 'seemed but a stone's throw away', he was
surely seeing far, far past Kintail, and on that compass bearing, there are only the Cuillin to stop your eyes drifting off
into Atlantic oblivion.

I daydreamed about Seton Gordon over a summit lunch.
I never met him, but I know several people who knew him
well, and I know no-one born to the Highlands and Islands
of Scotland and who feels for their native landscapes, who
does not hold his work in a kind of reverence. It is true that
he often romanticised. It is probably true that here and there
he was duped by sly kinsmen when he travelled in search
of the legends of the land. But he was a pioneer, a peerless
naturalist, a writer of limited gifts which he utilised to great
effect, so that now and again a paragraph would rise up in
the reader's eyes (like the cone of Cairn Toul from the Great
Moss) and make a sublime moment.

His greatest gift was to communicate his love for the
landscapes of the Highlands and Islands, especially the
Cairngorms and Skye, and for nature, especially the golden
eagle and ptarmigan. He emerged from the Victorian era;
not with a gun slung under his arm but with a telescope and

a camera. He was a trailblazer as a photographer, trauchling monstrous equipment up mountainsides, building hides, and coming home with plates of ptarmigan creeping in to a plateau nest, at a time when many people thought the word 'ptarmigan' was a misprint, but they could not imagine what for.

His two studies of a nesting golden eagle in *The Cairngorm Hills of Scotland* are beautiful photographic images even by today's standards. It is difficult to imagine the stir they created when they were published in 1925. It is worth pointing out that the title page refers to 'photographs taken by the Author and his Wife' but there is no explanation of whether she took the pictures of him, or whether she was as good as he was at wildlife. But you realise the kind of company you keep when you read in his introduction to *The Golden Eagle*:

> It is a long time ago – April, 1904 – since I photographed my first golden eagle's eyrie.

He could have been no more than seventeen. His first book appeared three years later. When he died, aged 90, in 1977, he left behind legions of disciples, people who had been persuaded that it was acceptable to love wild places and wild life because he had done so unabashed. Legions more, who never set foot on plateau or ridge nor eyeballed a brooding ptarmigan, were just grateful that all his life he put pen to paper. They knew their land, and learned to love it, vicariously.

He determined the course of other people's lives, notably that of Adam Watson who knew him from childhood and grew to become one of the most passionate, eloquent and tenacious of all the voices ever raised on behalf of the Cairngorms and their unique species of wildness. Seton Gordon seems to have filtered into my own mind by some kind of osmosis. I can't remember first hearing about him, nor can I remember first reading him, but I was probably a teenager wondering aloud about those names which spilled enticingly across the blackboard at school geography lessons, then hearing them from the lips of hoary old pipe-smoking creatures in queer breeks 'up the Clovy' which was my generation of Dundee-speak for the all-purpose pursuits to be found in the hills around Glen Clova. He did not tell me to go to the Cairngorms or Skye – no-one did – but when I found him rooted in both places, he became something of an anchor from which endeavours of my own might voyage. I have never lost the habit of reworking my way through the pages of those half dozen of his twenty-odd books which I hold dearest.

Seton Gordon was a man of his time. Occasionally his language falls quaintly on today's ears. Sometimes it wears the lineage of anglicised Gaelic, which may be an affectation, or it may be the way he consciously tried to make prose poetry. He was tall and thin and perpetually kilted. Those who climbed with him spoke of his slow and tireless stride and his ability to spellbind an audience even in the very last weeks of his life. By then, of course, he was living history, a moving swathe through time, and the Cairngorms he described was as much the one he inherited as the one he experienced.

If he should appear now, standing beside me by the summit cairn of Ben MacDhui, what would I say to him? I thought about it for a moment, then I fished out my copy of *The Cairngorm Hills of Scotland*, which now and again travels with me into the mountain midst which spawned it. I would point to a short paragraph from the chapter entitled 'Ben Mac Dhui: A Hill of Windy Acres', and ask him to read it, so that I could hear it in his own voice. It would not be a Scottish-sounding voice, for he was educated privately (which is rare in an Aberdeenshire farmer's son, I would guess, but there are those who say he had royal parentage and that explains his friends in high places and his gift of a telescope from the Prince of Wales when he was at Oxford …the only biography about him declined to investigate the rumours, and now – who cares?). What I would ask him to read is this:

> Dusk came, and in the still waters of Lochan Uaine of Ben Mac Dhui the clouds were mirrored. Beside the loch a few small stags grazed. There was a great restfulness about the high tops that evening, and in the calm air rose the crooning of the Dee as it flowed south through the Lairig a full 2000 feet below.

You have to have lingered there more than once to hear the crooning of the Dee from the summit of Ben MacDui.

I would seek out Loch Avon by way of Loch Etchachan, a descent of over 1000 feet. The nature of the land - that you can descend over 1000 feet to a loch which lies at 3100 feet, and on the way down you will feel the day warm as you slip out of reach of the plateau's rarefied taste in winds.

I think it was twenty years before that I last stood on the shore of Loch Etchachan. I had forgotten how big it was. Memory always shrinks the Cairngorms, because their scale is so exceptional in the context of the Scottish Highlands.

Every journey takes longer than you think. Even your eye is defeated by the shape and size of things. And I had quite forgotten the existence of Loch Etchachan Beag. Lochs like Loch Etchachan are for sitting beside, for being a rock on the shore, for giving it as much time as you can and see what rubs off. What rubbed off, after about half an hour of mindless rock impersonating, was a posse of swifts, which was hardly what I was expecting. They appeared high and from the direction of Beinn Mheadhoin, and in one of those moments of supreme confusion when you are unsure if the glasses have picked up something very small and very close or something much bigger and much further away (at such a moment on the Insh Marshes I once turned a dragonfly into an osprey). But no sooner had the glasses found them than my ears found them too, and nothing is confused with that devilish, raking voice. The flock of about thirty birds (it is no easy task counting a flock of flat-out swifts) banked towards the loch in a loose squadron, and for a quarter of an hour they strafed it almost to the water level although it was quite unclear to me what they were catching.

Slowly I began to realise that their numbers had thinned to a dozen, then quite suddenly there were none at all. It was as if the whole flock had never been.

I sat on, wonderfully aware of where I was sitting, how remote it suddenly felt from the 'crowded hours of human life'. Yet human life has rarely been richer, and still the September light put Midas shades on rock face and loch shore, and struck tiny headlights on miniature waves. A dozen hinds moved slowly over the lower slopes of Beinn Mheadhoin, and their backs and haunches were rimmed by it, and if Seton Gordon had reappeared then on my loch shore, offered me his telescope, and as I squinted at the haloed deer, told me legends of deer as fairy cattle, being milked by the good folk in the evening, I would have swallowed it all whole. Landscapes, not idle minds, are the begetters of legends, the spawning beds of myth. We simply pick them up where we find them lying around like shed ptarmigan feathers.

The deer drifted down to the loch, and thanks to the wind and my own rock-stillness we shared a shore for a while: I watched and they drank, until the matriarch of the herd looked directly at me across a quarter of a mile of water, muttered a gruff monosyllable which raised every drinking head, and then they all stared. No deer moved, beyond the flick of ears and the questioning of noses (I remembered the roe and the squirrel and smiled to myself at the memory). Two heads bent back to drinking, then two more, then another. The last to drink was the matriarch, but her head was up again almost at once. She was on to me, but she couldn't make my seated shape into what her nose was telling her. Unease won, she barked again, and led the way at a stiff trot back the way the herd had come.

The light on Beinn Mheadhoin grew magical. The deer crossed the lower slopes inkily, like rocks on the move uphill. Just above them the mountainside was something like the colour of yellowhammers. I rose and followed where the deer had gone, and with the day's long adjustment to the plateau air now complete, I climbed with a quite irresistible zest, high on oxygen. The broad crown of the summit reeled itself in almost without effort. I dropped the pack and looked round. In the late afternoon, the September goldening of the massif was complete. The crags above Loch Avon gleamed as if they were dull metal rather than granite, and the plateau of Cairn Gorm lay blissful and unwounded, as though the light had healed its every scar and blemish.

Bynack's weird 'Barns' looked almost within touching distance, and that wide spreadeagle of hill and moorland country from Glen Avon to Tomintoul which normally falls formidably on a watcher's eye, looked quilted and coy.

But there was no hiding place for the livid weal of Beinn a Bhuird's mountain road. The colossal bulk of its western slopes was curiously unsoftened by the light, or perhaps that was just my own prejudices at work for I consider that road to be one of the foulest intrusions wrought by man on mountain anywhere in the Highlands, which is no meagre claim to infamy.

Glen Derry restored the magic in the south, for the gold was only on its eastern flank. A deep black, that same ink shade as the contouring deer had spilled down the glen's western half from the stony torso of Derry Cairngorm. It was on that wondrous little upthrust ('little' is relative – 3788 feet would look astoundingly impressive in Sutherland, but wedged under and overtopped 500 feet by Ben MacDui is not the best place to pose for effect) that the light briefly worked its best trick. The hilltop was simply black, but yellow bars soared up the sky behind it. The mountain Gods were playing games, and I was all the audience they had.

I drained all the light I could from that afternoon and evening, staying high while the shadows shifted and grew pervasive, till the sky calmed down and yellow light turned quietly pale then gray and the lit innumerable hills in the north-east went out, one by one. It is a long shadow the Cairngorms massif throws at sunset. I watched the mountain throw it, saw it land and blacken the world of lesser landscapes. In the dusk I went down into the cold, still underworld of Loch Avon.

Underworld! Loch Avon lies at 2400 feet! But there is almost 2000 feet of mountainside to look up to, to swarm around the head of the loch, the armour-plated hull of the massif at its most inscrutable. I put my tent down where the river emerges from the loch, made a brew to wash down the curiously palatable tinned stew, then slid into my sleeping bag and watched the loch and the mountain blackness while the cup steamed in my hand. If there is a word for the spirit of well-being which unites such an hour and such a landscape and such a frame of mind, I have not encountered it yet. Perhaps is exists in old Gaelic, a question I could put to Seton Gordon if he turned up on my evening's shore.

I woke in the night, shivering. It was 3am. It is always 3am when you awake shivering in the night. I lit the stove for a few minutes, found another layer of clothing, put my jacket over it and went outside. A low mist lay along the trench of the loch. There was a thin coat of ice on the tent. The only sound was the river. There was no view in any direction. There were no mountains.

I stood quite still for perhaps ten minutes and thought of nothing at all. Then I remembered what I had wanted to do here. I had wanted to look from my tent to the Feith Buidhe to that spot a little distance away from Hell's Lum where I had paused the morning before, and wave to myself. When I had the chance I had forgotten, and now that I remembered, I couldn't see fifty yards. Still, the daft notion had provided the impetus for being here; whatever it takes, I told myself, whatever it takes.

The morning after, the September sun restored, the long walk down Glen Derry – the way out again; the welcome of pine trees, the incongruous shapes of black grouse in the branches, the scent of autumn on the air, the long road home. Always, the long road home, always the feeling of not-quite-repleteness, as though I have left something behind, a part of me that was present on the mountain, but now absent. That's what I go back for, every time, to reclaim that which has been left behind, but which does not travel beyond the shadow of the pines, which will not descend down into the crowded hours of human life.

Chapter Eleven

Caught in a Rut

THERE IS NOTHING a promotional tourist board film likes more than to film a running herd of red deer from the air. Overlay it with a soundtrack of lump-in-the-throat music, chuck in a couple of castles (usually the seats of chieftains who betrayed their own people and had them cleared to make way for sheep, then deer like the ones just filmed, but let it pass), strew a few clichés through the voice-over, and whatever you do, don't let either the sound or the fatal give-away shadow of the cameraman's helicopter give the game away. It was, after all, the cameraman's helicopter which persuaded the deer to run in the first place. A herd of red deer only runs when it is very alarmed. Few things can appear more alarming than a helicopter materialising up out of the Lairig Ghru, rising to just overhead, stopping in mid air, then when the deer run, the bellowing beast follows, overtakes, turns and comes at them head-on so that the whole herd changes direction.

The film plays on the fact that it is a beautiful thing to watch. The fact that deer's behaviour and the nature of the terrain where they stampede are wholly unnatural says as much about the kind of Highland Scotland tourism believes in as it does about what people have done to our deer and our landscape.

Gleann Quoich on a September evening, the yellow light

again, and all along the level terraces of the moraines above the river the deer congregate in their thousands. In the low sunlight, and with the long summer days of almost constant feeding behind them, the deer look good. The rut is just a few weeks away. They are in the best of condition. Right? Wrong.

There are far too many deer, and what you see, flattered by the September sun, is overcrowding, a red deer slum, with all the attendant problems of slum dwelling. The animals are undernourished and physically impoverished. And as a result, exactly the same can be said of their habitat. The only cause which is served by the status quo is the perverse economics of the sporting estate, where the deer is not a wild animal but a source of revenue.

Look again at the hordes lining the riverbanks of Gleann Quoich. The greatest kindness which we as a species could confer on the red deer as a species is to kill two out of every three where they stand, and repeat the process all across the Highlands. The result – in time, in time, for there is much to be done in the regeneration and restoration of habitat, and Highland habitats do not restore quickly – will be a restored race of red deer a third bigger than they are now, which is what they should be. They will also be restored as forest animals, which is what they should be, for the forest will have been restored to a state of health which can accommodate the restored deer herd. And what will the helicoptered cameraman do then for his clichés?

The trees and the deer are at their best when the one frames the other, because they belong, mutually.

There was an old October, this very glen, these very pines, afternoon sun on a quiet clearing in the trees. I had been there a long hour, licking my wounds after a joust with

Beinn a'Bhuird and its road, my first and my last until the road is broken up and re-seeded, the scar persuaded to heal. Then the wood around me began to explode. There was the stamping of impetuous feet, the metallic clatter of locking antlers, then the grating throb of a bellowing stag, that symphonic discord which announced the impending arrival in the clearing of one of nature's set pieces – the red deer rut. Like anyone who spends much of life among mountains, I had seen and heard the rut many times, but I had never witnessed it – or even contemplated what it might look like – in a setting of trees. The fundamental difference, I know now, is that in the forest is announces itself while it is still invisible, so that its approaching tensions affect all in its path, which on this occasion included me. I dared not move because of what I might miss, yet for the first time in my life I knew fear in the presence of red deer.

Why fear? The unknown. I did not know how they would react to my presence or if they would even notice it, whether a stag in trees would react the same way as out on the open hill, or respond to his ancient terrain by defending it against all intrusion, no matter how many legs the intruder had.

Hinds entered the arena of trees first, and at a placid trot, which had the effect of devaluing the ferocity of the stag's overture. I had anticipated a wild-eyed, strewn panic, forgetting in the disturbing moments of their advance that it is simply not in the nature of the hinds to be panicked by the stags' jealousies and jousts. Here, as on the open hill, they wandered at will, and the stags followed them.

The hinds, fourteen of them, strayed to the river and stopped to drink, while the stags' battleground shifted unnervingly behind my back. I realised then that I sat between the stags and the hinds, a knowledge which did nothing to mitigate my discomfort. I was nakedly aware of the fact that they were in their element and – at least as far as they were concerned – I was not.

A tremendous clash of antlers close behind, the soft thunder of heather-happed hooves. A young stag burst in on the hinds' arena not ten feet to my left. There uncoiled then, the same distance to my right, the rawest, most awesome noise I have ever heard this side of a snow avalanche. My head jerked right, involuntary contravention of my self-imposed demands for stillness at all costs...the master stag!

He was peat-black, hoary-muzzled, thick-chested, high-headed, wide-antlered, barrel-necked, and with the wind working mercifully in my favour, he stank. He advanced four slow strides towards the young stag now thrusting his attentions on one straying hind. But at the sound of the master's first quickening stride, he turned abruptly to face his rival. Then, with a clear gesture like a shying horse he swerved off with a fast sideways twist. He conceded.

By the time the master stag was halfway across the clearing, the young beast was in retreat and heading for an alley in the trees, a path which, by a trick of fate or some kindly gesture from some God-of-the-deer, propelled him head-on towards the flank of the strayed hind. She, with all options removed, ran before him, so that in his hour of defeat, and quite involuntarily, he had gleaned the first bride of his first harem.

The master stag slowed to negotiate more trees, but if he had contemplated pursuit, a bark and purposeful stride from the matriarchal hind stopped him. He bellowed again, then turned to outflank the drift of his hinds back the way he had come. They went anyway, and he followed, honour - or whatever – satisfied, but with only thirteen hinds at his disposal. The whole episode, from first inklings to last gasp, had taken perhaps a minute-and-a-half.

In the stunned and sunny silence which followed, I sat in a kind of privileged shock. I saw nothing, heard nothing, sensed nothing. The deer, if they had noticed me at all, had treated me as they would treat a fallen pine cone, a scrap of litter on the forest floor. I snapped out of it only when the tree where I sat began to rain on me. I know that rain. I looked up, grinning at the bark-spitting quest of a tree creeper.

A friend of mine, a forester, once told me, 'A forest is not a forest without deer.'

I now had all the vindication I would ever need of that statement. The pinewood is the deer's place. It is our place to put them back where they belong. In the absence of natural predators – and the reintroduction of wolves is some distance away yet – we have to ensure that there are not too many deer for the good of the pinewoods, and for that matter that there are not too many nor too few deer for their own good. It is not a complex equation. But those landowners who hold too many deer so that they can be shot for profit keep a stranglehold on the possibility of progress.

Awareness grows. In the Cairngorms there is wider recognition than ever before that what is at risk is unique. But the threats grow too, an ominous if uncoordinated amalgam of tourism, the leisure industry and landowners unwilling to acknowledge the twentieth century even as it draws to a close.

A notable exception is Rothiemurchus, whose own visitors guide says:

Control of deer numbers by man is essential as most of their natural predators such as wolves now only roam in the wildlife park. This ensures the wellbeing of the population which is maintained in balance with the environment. The population is held at a level which does not cause excessive damage to naturally regenerating pine seedlings by browsing. Deer management is essential for the conservation of both the pine forest and the deer herd...

There is a first commandment of Cairngorms land management enshrined in that simple philosophy. And it works, it works!

Chapter twelve

The Sanctity of Silence

AGAIN AND AGAIN in the last few years, whenever the Cairngorms crop up in my life – which is often – I go back in my mind to that silence, the one which David Craig and I strolled into on the Moine Mhor. It is so often a place where the skies fill up with winds, winds which can flatten a man (it happened to me thirteen times in one day between Gleann Einich and Coire an Lochain), but on the day of the silence, we walked in nothing but the thinnest breeze. Dave and I recognised in the same instant that our feet made the only sound. The wind had gone, and in its place it left a wondrous symbolic nothing. I think of it as my life's one sacred moment.

It takes a landscape of rare distinction to broach casks of silence and let it flow. It is doubtless a component of the Australian outback, of deserts, of moons. But mostly, when it happens, it is the preserve of the Arctic. The high plateau of the Cairngorms is, in its every characteristic, Arctic. It is therefore fragile, rare, precious beyond price, and in the context of the landscapes of Britain and much of Europe, it is unique.

Unique. That word again. I want it re-invented so that it falls on all our ears as something startling, which is what it is. My dictionary defines it thus:

Having no like or equal

What higher accolade can there be? What more can you ask of a landscape than that it confers on your life a single moment of sanctity? Unique. Unique. Unique. It is what the Cairngorms are. Among our mountain landscapes, they have no like or equal. Recognition of that status should thrill us. It should be enough to persuade any self-esteeming society that here is a place to revere, for its own unique sake. Here, as surely as in mid-ocean or tropical rainforest or Africa's great plains, is a place where natural forces work at their extremities. The fitting, dignified, civilised response from a society which cares about where and how it lives would be to give nature its head, stand back, wonder, admire, marvel. Above all – to safeguard the uniqueness.

Instead, society reserves for the Cairngorms a unique contempt.

Huge parcels of the massif and its pinewood remnants are bought and sold on whims. Serious nature conservation intent has been either discouraged or conspired against. Landowning practice locks the landscape into timewarps of anti-nature. Red deer saturation inhibits the restoration of every natural habitat from the pinewoods to the plateau, all in the name of the most loathed euphemism in the Highlands – 'sporting estate'. As a land use in such a land-scape it is as ignoble as it is unworthy. Anyone with a big enough bank balance or persuasive enough connections can become a landowner in the Cairngorms. No question is asked about their intentions or their track records in land-scape conservation, or how long they plan to stay. It is a conspicuous truth that among the private landowners in the Cairngorms, the only ones with a track record to take some

pride in are the Grants of Rothiemurchus, a family attach-
ment to the same piece of ground which reaches back
several centuries. And Seton Gordon records this unique
item of pedigree:

> Here, beside Coire Odhar, the people of
> Rothiemurchus formerly had their summer
> sheilings, and the laird with his wife and family
> were in the habit of accompanying them to their
> summer home. Indeed, in this remote place, one
> of the Grants of Rothiemurchus was born, and
> took his name, Corrour Grant, from the Corrie.

It is a far cry from being named after the corrie in which you
were born to the fitted kitchen manufacturer from the
English Midlands who was one of the more recent fly-by-
night landowners of Glen Feshie. He did not stay long. If
you can't stand the cold, get back in the kitchen. And at Mar
Lodge, another landowner turned up who had bought the
estate because his wife wanted royal neighbours. Yet legally,
neither of these people did anything wrong. There was
nothing to stop them. There is still nothing to stop it hap-
pening again.

We profess as a society to know the worth of heritage. Yet
we preside over the lowest ebb of the Cairngorms landscape
since the last ice age finished with it. Its downward spiral of
degradation sustains its momentum fuelled by landowner
complacency and the meddling of local and national poli-
tics. Over much of the mountain massif, nature is in retreat.
Yet how eagerly it would advance if it was given so much as
half a chance. It takes the investment of energy and
resources to keep nature in check in a landscape as natural

as the Cairngorms. No expense is spared to batten it down, close it in, stamp it out.

By any reasonable comparison of what has been and what exists now, Glen Feshie is derelict, dying on its feet. Yet the means to save it, to resuscitate nature and let it live and breathe again was on offer, a bid for ownership by the RSPB and the John Muir Trust. The RSPB has demonstrated at Abernethy that it can unite its energies and resources to the breadth of its imagination. At one extreme it contests the political dogfight to win its arguments. At the other, it has liberated Abernethy. It operates with the confidence generated by a membership of one million, which makes it politically formidable. The John Muir Trust is young and small-time by comparison, but it aims as high, and would have learned a great deal in a short time from a partnership with the RSPB in a Cairngorms setting.

Both organisations have a purity of purpose, and accountability to a membership of real people. Their alliance was a solution to the ills of Glen Feshie on a plate. If the Government had wanted to demonstrate it had the wellbeing of the natural environment at heart (but then, when did it ever?), here was political manna from heaven. But the National Heritage Memorial Fund refused a modest funding request and the path was smoothed for the mysterious Will Woodland Trust to buy the estate. Pious pledges from the lawyers of anonymous directors prevailed. It is a naive fool who would believe anything other than that landowning interests wanted to ensure that conservation principles did not dictate the future of Glen Feshie. There are few naive fools left among those who fight for the future of the Cairngorms.

When the National Trust for Scotland was given twice as

much money as the RSPB/JMT bid for Glen Feshie had sought, this time to buy the huge Mar Lodge estate, it was difficult to contain cynicism. The NTS has a poor and much criticised record of mountain estate management, but its links with both the Scottish Landowners Federation and the then Conservative Government run deep. Add to that the bonds forged in old schools and regiments and you have an all-but-impenetrable network of friends in high places. And these too are brought to bear on the forces of unfettered nature in the Cairngorms.

The Conservative Government further constrained the hopes of serious Cairngorms-wide progress by hamstringing its agency, Scottish Natural Heritage, with impotent dead-weights of bureaucracy. The role of SNH should be self-evident – to champion the cause of nature and landscape. But landscape champions must stem from within the landscape, so that they can convince their own kin, their own people, the true owners of the land.

The Government also created the Cairngorms Partnership, a laborious talking shop of all the mountain's vested interests – a forum which guarantees that radical voices will be smothered, radical solutions shouted down, in the perpetual quest for that holiest of bureaucratic grails, compromise.

But compromise has given the Cairngorms what it has now, which is insidious dereliction. The devastating power of the compromise culture is seen in the response of conservation organisations to the preposterous proposal for a funicular railway on the Cairn Gorm ski slopes, not a funicular railway – a gondola! You can almost hear the fearful voice at work...'Mustn't be seen to be negative...must make a positive contribution. Propose a less damaging alternative, eh? Damage limitation...that's the answer!'

No. It is not the answer.

Not in the Cairngorms.

Not in that priceless Arctic fragment.

Not in that harbourer of silence.

Not in the one unique landscape in our country.

Damage limitation will not do. Only restoration will do.

Heal the landscape wounds! That is the only cause worth fighting for in the Cairngorms, absolutely the only one. Conservation on a scale conservationists have not yet contemplated – that should be the quest in place of compromise.

The best piece of nature writing I have ever read, the American Aldo Leopold's much quoted *Sand County Almanac*, observed:

> The practices we now call conservation are, to a large extent, local alleviations of biotic pain. They are necessary, but they must not be confused with cures.

The quest in the Cairngorms must be for cures. The implication of Leopold's truism is that there is a great difference between conservation and cure. In the Cairngorms – uniquely! – it is the immensity of difference which matters. There is nothing like the landscape of the Cairngorms, and if we seek cures, then ski-ing can play no part in it, and neither can the pot-shot plaything priorities of landowners with Victorian chips on their shoulders. The cure for the Cairngorms necessitates removing both these, for they are the forces which act contrary to the natural regeneration of every indigenous habitat, the forces which blight the wellbeing of the mountain massif, the forces of anti-nature.

Cloud-cuckoo land, right?

Unhinged from the real world, right?

Or as a Scottish Landowners Federation spokesman remarked on radio:

> 'There is an awful lot of chasing moonbeams among conservationists in the Cairngorms. Things aren't really that bad.'

Ah, the voice of reason, and delivered as always in cut-glass public school tones, which are meant to reassure us. We are not assured.

It doesn't reassure nature either, and neither does a gondola. The only thing which holds conservation in check in the Cairngorms is the limit of its own ambition. If it includes a gondola in the northern corries of Cairn Gorm where dwelt the spirit of the high and lonely places, then it is certainly not interested in 'cures'. The effects of ski development stain the Cairngorms massif far beyond the plateau and northern corries of Cairn Gorm. One more new development will beget others. As long as the principle is established – that development in the Cairngorms is permissible – then there will be those who will seek to develop it further. Developer ambitions have cast envious eyes on Beinn a'Bhuird, the Lairig Ghru, the Garbh Choire and plateau of Braeriach for years now, and have been held back only by sustained rearguard actions. No-one has told them 'never', because there is no law protecting the Cairngorms which says 'never'.

So the cure begins with the removal of all ski-ing development from the Cairngorms for all time, the closing of Cairn Gorm itself for say, a hundred years, which should permit healing at nature's pace. Ski-ing can flourish in many places in Scotland. I hope it does. But in the Cairngorms the landscape is too precious and too rare to permit it. As long as it is a component of what the Cairngorms landscape has become, its commercial appetite will grow and nature and its silences will wither.

The chairman of the Cairngorm Chairlift Company defended the funicular railway recently with a familiar announcement: 'The economy of the Highlands is yoked to tourism.' It is a half-truth, and it is truer now than it used to be, that is no cause for celebration, for it is the most thoughtless and demanding of industries at its worst, and its worst lies perilously close to the foot of the Cairn Gorm ski slopes.

Yet conservation – cure-seeking – on a Cairngorms-wide scale offers untold employment prospects, recruiting from a local workforce, teaching real skills, creating jobs for all time which are not dependent on the weather. The only reason why there has been no study of the prospects for yoking the economy of the Highlands from Speyside to Deeside to conservation is because vested interests fear it.

But it is the way forward. A Scottish Parliament, with powers to establish that in some places (and the Cairngorms is at the top of that short list) land management means nature conservation as first priority, and a conservation movement which dares beyond its wildest dreams...none of these things is beyond us. Nor is far-reaching reform of land ownership which insists on control over who can buy, how much they can buy, and what they will do with it.

A cure for the Cairngorms is within our grasp, as is a sanctuary for its silences.

Chapter thirteen

The Heart of the Cairngorms

THE DOOR TO the Cairngorms was opened to me the day I was born. My parents' home was the meagrest of houses, a post-war corporation prefab in Dundee, but it was – crucially – in the last street in town. Across the road was farmland, fields which climbed, and climbed north to a crest which contemplated the Sidlaw Hills, and I can only imaging from the path I followed that I was born facing north. The Sidlaws, and occasionally the Angus Glens beyond, were for childhood and early teenage years, when it was enough to be in such places without questioning why or setting objectives. But there would come the day when being there meant climbing – boots, a rucksack, and something to keep out the rain. Glen Clova and Glen Doll became the holy ground.

I don't remember dates and places, occasions and faces with any reliability. I don't remember the circumstances of my first ascent of Jock's Road with any clarity. But I have in my mind a single souvenir of the day, one image of the world which lies beyond Angus from the crown of that happy highway between the hills of home and Braemar under the Cairngorms. It is of one bewilderingly big coalescence of mountain shapes, white to the waist when the rest of the world's mountain distance looked blue. I think it was late summer, and nothing had prepared me for the possibility of summer snow.

It is as if all the detail of that hour has been consciously blurred and made irrelevant so that its one shining and pivotal moment could survive the years. I was probably on my own, I think I had my first car, I think I turned from the top of Jock's Road and went back into Clova in a state of disbelief. I suddenly remembered a friend of my parents, Dave Fleming, showing me a photograph of winter in Torridon (he travelled there addictively, almost ritually, all his adult life) and marvelling aloud to me that such a scene could occur in Scotland when it looked so much more like Switzerland.

I would tell him about this new summer snow I had found. I was not at all sure he would believe me. There was a difference in this Cairngorms snow, apart from the fact that it had fallen in August. It seemed to lie so eternally horizontal, whereas the Torridon winter snow had been spired and spiked, vertical stuff; deep and showy, not shallow, blunt and bare.

I was nineteen, perhaps twenty. In the intervening thirty years, I have learned a little more about that horizontal snow, more about that mountain coalescence, more about its Arctic repertoire of snows.

Most of us know snow as a here-today-gone-tomorrow creature with no appetite for endurance. It is not the Cairngorms' way with snow, not the Arctic way. In the high Cairngorms, on corrie walls and gullies which face away from the sun, snow endures. From time to time in the mountain's story, snow endures long enough to grow old, older than people so that a single snowfield – usually one snowfield in particular in the Garbh Choire – outlives living memory. Living memory at any one time might span a century if you allow the oldest inhabitant's memory of a parent's accounts. What are we to make of one-hundred-year-old snow? I think of sitting high in the Garbh Choire in midwinter with the snow falling thickly, watching a single flake selected from the grey mass and following it until it lands, thinking that where it lies, it might outlive my grandchildren, if I ever have any, crushed and compacted by tons of older snows beneath, younger snows above, but still itself.

It is an astonishing place, the Garbh Choire, four corries in one, and none of them mundane. The great snowfield is in the Garbh Choire Mor, a wild upper chamber slung from the rim of the headwall, like a martin's nest. Snow needs shelter to lie behind to build a great depth. The snow winds which flail the Great Moss find none until they hit the Garbh Choire Mor, at 4000 feet, and there they dive down the abyss and their snows pile high. In midwinter the snowscape of the whole Garbh Choire can instil fear, its massive smoothness as surreal as it is untrustworthy. But a mild spring and an easy summer can whittle the mass back to a few clinging square yards, and in the newly bared rock at the edge of the snows, plants and mosses rush out, and make what they can of sunlight and wind before winter turns up again, as it usually does in the early autumn. The September snowfield is brown-black and stony, pitted with gravel, five or six feet deep, more boulder-like than snow-like. But it clings, and when the new snows come, it clings still, and grows like itself again. But for a few weeks, just as the ptarmigan are beginning to change from summer to autumn moult, they are the colour and broken textures of the half-caste birds...bouldery, gravelly, snowy, the plumage of the ptarmigan between summer and winter. Somehow, nature has taught the ptarmigan awareness of the fact. They flock to the old snows to roost.

There is an old August among my own repertoire of Cairngorms snows, the day hot, the Feith Buidhe dawdling down from its tiny lochan towards the crags above Loch Avon, and near where it tumbles over the rim, I found a wedge of old snow twenty feet thick. It had built up over a ledge and against a crag, and where ledge met crag the meltwater had made a tunnel high enough to walk through, albeit with a bit of a crouch. I went in, and at once the warm day was cool. I stopped in the middle of the tunnel and sat down, my back to the rock, my face to the curve of hollowed out snow. With my shoulder against the rock, my outstretched hand and arm could reach the snow.

This, I thought, is what it is to be under the skin of the mountain. This is how the snowbed mosses live for almost all of their lives, storing life enough under the snow until – years from now – the snowfields shrink enough to grant them an audience with the overworld.

The pink rock was darkened the colour of dulled blood by the seeping water. In a day like this, how much of the snow would melt away, how much higher and wider would the tunnel grow? How many more scraps of moss and other green things would be liberated?

The old snow was not smooth on the inside of the tunnel wall, but scalloped, worn away in gentle grooves with grimy, gritty edges. Tiny red spiders ran here and there, mostly upside down. Are they moss-and-darkness dwellers when the snows clamp down again, part-time troglodytes? Or surface dwellers unhappy in sunlight?

How quickly the tunnelled existence wipes out the sense of the mountain, implants instead the air of something subterranean. This is as close as I will ever get to something resembling the home of the Wells of Dee, a dark hollow chamber beneath the mountain skin where the raw materials of a mountain burn are woven beyond the scope of all eyes and made lucid for the bubbling entry into the light, there to make music and waterfalls and slake thirsts.

What can I weave to take with me out of here, bubbling back up into the light, some new lucidity to flourish across the plateau? It is the knowledge of the heart of the Cairngorms, where water meets rock and reforms, and succours all life; where lifeblood is made and seeps darkly down a rockface inside the mountain; where primeval things move in uncanny darkness and sounds echo weirdly like water in a cave. Is that rhythmic dripping the echo of a beating granitic pulse?

If the shape of the planet makes sense from the plateau, the shape of the mountain makes sense from here. I feel I could contour all the way round the mountain from here, tunnelled under its skin, circumnavigating its skull between rock and snow, a subterranean journey at 4000 feet. But the tunnel is only twenty yards long, and it dips to the south, and threatens to tip you out by way of its slithery rock surface, out on to the mountainside, bouncing and broken into Loch Avon 1500 feet below. That glimpse of the heart is enough, and all I need. I am no troglodyte. It has begun to feel uneasy, confined, walled in, the antithesis of all that makes the Cairngorms landscape what it is. The landscape is defined by the outside of the skin, not the inside, because it needs space in which to be defined, more space than a tunnel has to offer, even space in a tunnel of years-old snow.

I clambered out, stood blinking in the sunlight, patted the old wet and hard mass of the snow and climbed back for the plateau where the waters of Feith Buidhe were reassuringly lucid, fully formed, un-echoing. Still, I told myself, it was good to be tunnelled in briefly and guess at the scheme of things walled deep inside the mountain.

Acknowledgements

Thanks to David Craig for the Cailleach days and his poem *The Height of the Great Moss*. And I acknowledge with gratitude the debt I owe in the Cairngorms to the writing of Seton Gordon.

Select Bibliography

CRAIG, David   *Landmarks*, Cape 1996

CRUMLEY, Jim   *A High and Lonely Place*, Cape 1991

                    Among Mountains, Mainstream 1993

GORDON, Seton   *The Cairngorm Hills of Scotland*, Cassell 1925

                    The Golden Eagle, Collins 1955 and Melven Press 1980

MAXWELL, Gavin   *Raven Seek Thy Brother*, Longmans 1968

SHEPHERD, Nan   *The Living Mountain*, Aberdeen University Press 1981 and Canongate 1996

WATSON, Adam & Nethersole-Thompson, Desmond

                    The Cairngorms, Collins 1974 and Aberdeen University Press 1981

Other books by Jim Crumley:

The Heart of Mull
The Heart of Skye
Gulfs of Blue Air
The Road and the Miles
Among Mountains
Among Islands
A High and Lonely Place
Waters of the Wild Swan
Badgers on the Highland Edge
Discovering the Pentland Hills
Royal Mile

With photographer Colin Baxter:
St Kilda
West Highland Landscape
Glencoe – Monarch of Glens
Shetland – Land of the Ocean
Portrait of Edinburgh